John Marshall's
Constitutionalism

SUNY Series in American Constitutionalism

Robert J. Spitzer, editor

John Marshall's Constitutionalism

Clyde H. Ray

SUNY PRESS

Published by State University of New York Press, Albany

For information, contact State University of New York Press, Albany, NY
www.sunypress.edu

Library of Congress Cataloging-in-Publication Data

Names: Ray, Clyde, author.
Title: John Marshall's constitutionalism / Clyde H. Ray.
Description: New York : State University of New York Press, [2019] | Series:
    SUNY series in American constitutionalism | Includes bibliographical
    references and index.
Identifiers: LCCN 2018033270 | ISBN 9781438474410 (hardcover : alk. paper) |
    ISBN 9781438474403 (pbk. : alk. paper) | ISBN 9781438474427 (ebook)
Subjects: LCSH: Marshall, John, 1755–1835—Political and social views. |
    Judges—United States—Biography. | Constitutional law—United States. |
    Constitutional history—United States. | United States. Supreme
    Court—Biography. | United States—Politics and government—History.
Classification: LCC KF8745.M3 R39 2019 | DDC 342.73—dc23
LC record available at https://lccn.loc.gov/2018033270

10 9 8 7 6 5 4 3 2 1

A society grows great when old men plant trees whose shade they know they shall never sit in.

—Greek proverb

Contents

Acknowledgments

This book would not have been written without the many teachers, colleagues, and friends who have helped me better understand John Marshall. I am grateful, first of all, to Michael Lienesch for his careful criticism and editorial comments on the dissertation out of which this book emerged. Mike has been a patient and generous mentor since the very beginning of my time at the University of North Carolina, and his extensive feedback on the prose and arguments of this book were invaluable. In addition, Jeff Spinner-Halev, Susan Bickford, Sandy Kessler, and Kevin McGuire provided detailed suggestions that helped clarify and strengthen my arguments concerning Marshall's political thought. Other individuals deserve credit for helping this work along in more informal conversations. In particular, I am deeply appreciative to Luke Perez, Luke Sheahan, and John-Paul Petrash for their intellectually enriching advice and good friendship.

Over several years, the University of North Carolina at Chapel Hill, Duke University, Western Carolina University, and the Institute for Humane Studies provided important financial and creative support for my research on this book. Without their help, the writing of this book would have taken a much longer amount of time. SUNY Press has paved the production of this work with smooth efficiency. Michael Rinella and Rafael Chaiken have provided able editorial assistance, and the book has benefited greatly from the feedback of three anonymous reviewers who commented on an earlier version of this manuscript.

Throughout the production of this book, indeed throughout life, I have been blessed with the support of a wonderful family. For years, my wife, Gladys, and sons, William and Ambrose, lived alongside the day-to-day life of a writer—to say nothing of a graduate student. For their ongoing encouragement, understanding, and love, I will always be grateful. I dedicate this work to them.

Chapters 1 and 2 of this book draw from two earlier and slightly different articles. Chapter 1 is based on "John Marshall, *Marbury v. Madison*, and the Construction of Constitutional Legitimacy," *Law, Culture and the Humanities* (forthcoming in print). Chapter 2 draws from "John Marshall, *McCulloch v. Maryland*, and the Concept of Constitutional Sovereignty," *Perspectives on Political Science* 47, no. 2 (2018): 65–77 (www.tandfonline. com). I am grateful to the publishers of these journals for allowing me to share revised versions of these pieces with readers of this volume.

Introduction

John Marshall and the American Constitution

Seated on the ground floor of the United States Supreme Court, the oversized statue of Chief Justice John Marshall is a mute reminder of a figure whose opinions and career most shaped the nation's judiciary. Like many of the monuments in the Capitol, the sculpture of Marshall is at once solid and remote, a bronze testament to both the greatness of his mind and the distance separating his time from our own.[1] His legal opinions, still read by most students of American law, remind us of his achievement in establishing the Court as a coequal branch of government.[2] In prose by turns sober and rousing, his words impress us with the strength of mind that shaped the rule of law into the hallmark of American government it represents today. But it would be a mistake to believe that Marshall's words are merely of historical importance, too far removed in time and place to guide Americans' contemporary conversations about the Constitution. Like Marshall, we continue to tie the Constitution's authority to the ongoing project of creating a more perfect union. In fact, Marshall's political thought has a great deal to teach Americans today.

This book is an investigation of that political thought. At the outset, it is important to distinguish its purpose from the many existing studies of Marshall's legal legacy. If ever a Mount Rushmore of Supreme Court justices is built, surely his face would be the first to be chiseled. He "has done more to establish the Constitution of the United States on sound construction than any other man living," President John Quincy Adams once wrote.[3] Nearly a century later, Woodrow Wilson was even more effusive in his praise of Marshall in a lecture to the students of Columbia University: "By common consent the most notable and one of the most statesman like figures in our whole judicial history is the figure of John Marshall," he declared. A master of "the fundamental conceptions which have enlightened all great lawyers in the administration of law," Wilson continued, "Marshall may be said to have created for us the principles of interpretation that have governed our national development."[4] Nor has Marshall's legal legacy been praised by Presidents alone. "If American law were to be represented by a single figure," Justice Oliver Wendell Holmes once rhapsodized, "sceptic and worshipper alike would agree without dispute that the figure could be one alone, and that one, John Marshall."[5] So we have been told, and so we believe. Yet in spite of his prominence in the realm of legal discourse, Marshall's political thought remains a subject of surprisingly little scholarly attention. This neglect is unfortunate, because Americans continue to grapple with many of the same issues of constitutional theory Marshall confronted. Thus, an engagement with Marshal's thought offers more than a better appreciation of perhaps our most important Supreme Court justice. It also speaks to and clarifies many of the questions and debates Americans continue to have regarding the Constitution.

Of course, the broad outlines of Marshall's political views are familiar to most students of the founding era. When it came to everyday politics, his beliefs were fairly straightforward: an unwavering commitment to the Federalist Party of Washington and Adams, a strong national government, and a robust, relatively unhampered market economy are among its trademarks. But the political philosophy underlying these principles—especially as it related to the fledgling role of the Constitution in the nation—is terrain that remains largely unexplored. Underneath Marshall's apparently uncompromising beliefs lies a larger political theory neither uniformly liberal nor republican but tethered above all to the authority of the Constitution. And just as it was the centerpiece of his thinking, so too he hoped it might become the guidepost for Americans with their own diverse political philosophies.

To some extent, the reasons for neglecting Marshall's political theory make sense. Marshall's opinions addressed timely political controversies rather than timeless principles of political theory. Unlike other members of the founding generation, he did not drink deeply from the wells of abstract political philosophy. Consumed instead with details of disputes, parties, and resolutions, little space remained for the detached speculation and high philosophy that we sometimes find in the writings of contemporaries such as James Madison and Thomas Jefferson.[6] Today, Marshall is remembered as a patriot, politician, diplomat, and judge, but not as a political philosopher. Nevertheless, his writings were inevitably both political and theoretical, insofar as he addressed timely controversies as well as timeless themes of political thought. For this reason, he deserves to be considered an important contributor to the history of American political thought.

To understand Marshall the political thinker, we should have some acquaintance with Marshall the man, for his rustic and frugal early life inevitably shines through his writing. He was born to Thomas Marshall and Mary Randolph Keith in 1755 in Fauquier County, Virginia, at that time a frontier community nestled in the Blue Ridge Mountains. Perhaps because of his rank in the family—he was the eldest of fifteen children— from an early age he cut a levelheaded and unaffected figure. Despite serving in the American Revolution and maintaining a lifelong admiration for George Washington, Marshall never indulged delusions of political grandeur. Instead, the study of law suited his practical, down-to-earth character, and following the Revolution he attended the lectures of Judge George Wythe at the College of William and Mary before being admitted to the Virginia bar and beginning his own private practice. And in such a private situation he may very well have remained, had not his reputation in legal circles led him to be nominated and elected to various positions in state government, including the General Assembly and State Executive Council. In 1788, his reputation for impartiality as well as his status as a war hero won him election to the Virginia Ratifying Convention of 1788, where he defended the proposed federal Constitution against such opponents as the formidable Patrick Henry, while also articulating his earliest public statements on the virtues of an independent judiciary.

Eventually, Marshall's devotion to order, property rights, and the restraints imposed by the rule of law led him to leave behind Virginia politics and a lucrative law practice. In 1797, he accepted an appointment by President John Adams to serve as an ambassador to France, where he defended the administration's policy of neutrality in what came to be known as the "XYZ" Affair. Buoyed by newfound national popularity in the aftermath of the negotiations, he reluctantly ran for and was elected to the House of Representatives in 1799, where his moderation and statesmanship distinguished him from partisan zealots on both sides of the political aisle. To the chagrin of Federalist Party leaders, Marshall was never a firebrand on behalf of his party's agenda, and perhaps for that reason his career in Congress proved short-lived. In 1800, he left Congress to serve as Secretary of State of the United States, his last official post before the one that would define his legacy.

On January 20, 1801, Adams nominated Marshall to the United States Supreme Court. Confirmed one week later, he took his seat on February 4. It was an office he would come to dominate: of the more than 1,000 cases he presided over as Chief Justice, he penned 519 opinions. Over the next three decades, his legal prowess was on display in his authorship of major constitutional opinions that helped define the document's role in the new nation. In cases such as *Marbury v. Madison* (1803), *McCulloch v. Maryland* (1819), and *Cohens v. Virginia* (1821) he empowered national authority; in cases like *Fletcher v. Peck* (1810), *Dartmouth College v. Woodward* (1819), and *Ogden v. Saunders* (1827) he defended property rights and the sanctity of private contracts; and in cases such as *Gibbons v. Ogden* (1824) he laid the legal foundations for a national economy. But perhaps Marshall's greatest contribution was the informal influence he wielded during his tenure. As Chief Justice, he took pains to build the prestige and influence of the Supreme Court, a body that political leaders and everyday citizens looked down on as weak and ineffective. On his watch, justices dined and lived together, donned uniform black robes for the first time, and began the norm of writing majority and minority (as opposed to seriatim) opinions. Alongside Marshall's written opinions, these personal touches—reinforced by his agreeable if austere personality—were pivotal in transforming the Court into a national institution. By the time he died, on July 6, 1835, the Supreme Court had achieved the prestige it still holds in the American political system.

Over the years, both Marshall and the volumes of opinions he left behind have been the subject of much scholarship. Interpretations vary widely, from the hagiographic to the cynical. Some have painted his life in grand and sweeping strokes, portraying his career as one of almost mythic accomplishment. Among the most famous of such panegyrics is Senator Albert Beveridge's multivolume *Life of John Marshall*, which portrays Marshall in a highly sympathetic light as a legal and political giant during his own lifetime and a national hero after his death.[7] Even more admiring interpretations have followed, emphasizing his decisive contribution in securing individual rights and legitimizing national power, as well as his self-conscious avoidance of the narrow political squabbles of his day. In these interpretations, Marshall was "the Great Chief Justice," the Constitution's most stalwart defender.[8] As one admiring biographer recently concluded, "Above all, Marshall's Court gave the American people—'We the people'—a means of redress against tyranny by federal, state, and local government."[9]

Other scholars have taken a more critical view of Marshall, often by situating him as a central player in early party politics. On these accounts, Marshall was the Federalist par excellence who used his position on the Supreme Court as a covert means to promote the party's policies. In these interpretations, Thomas Jefferson's devotion to decentralized authority and popular sovereignty met its match in Marshall, whose more subtle loyalties to the Federalist Party consistently led him to endorse strong central authority and separation of powers.[10] Look past his pretensions of upholding the Constitution and the rule of law, these authors argue, and one will see the authentic Marshall: the "ardent Federalist," loyal to the end to Washington, Adams, and the principles of national consolidation they championed.[11]

In contrast to those who either exalt or decry Marshall's political impact, other scholars have emphasized his legal legacy, notably his approach to constitutional interpretation. Yet here again scholars differ widely. For some, Marshall's chief contributions to legal theory are his fidelity to the rule of law and the words of the Constitution. His entire body of work, summarizes William Draper Lewis, shows "that he adhered closely to the words of the Constitution." Indeed, in his concentration on the constitutional text, "Marshall was the strictest of strict constructionists; and as a necessary result, his opinions are practically devoid of theories of government, sovereignty, and the rights of man."[12] Others have drawn very different conclusions, arguing that he expanded the power of the federal judiciary far beyond the limits set by the text of the Constitution.[13] These more critical appraisals point to opinions in cases such as *McCulloch*, which one recent writer has submitted as Exhibit A of Marshall's "aggressive nationalism."[14] Yet on one point most of these interpretations agree: that Marshall was the first in a long line of thinkers who defined the character of American constitutional law. As Supreme Court justice Benjamin Cardozo once declared, Marshall "gave to the constitution of the United States the impress of his own mind; and the form of our constitutional law is what it is, because he moulded it . . . in the fire of his own intense convictions."[15]

Compared to these political and legal analyses, political theorists have had little to say recently about John Marshall, and none brings his thought into conversation with contemporary political theory. His peripheral role in American political thought is unfortunate, because his opinions in fact have much to say about many of the themes and debates that occupy such theorists. By returning to his thought in light of these debates, we can better contextualize these discussions within our own political and legal history. But more than of mere historical interest, Marshall's political thought can still teach us a great deal about the bases for the Constitution's authoritative status in the twenty-first century. As prevalent as social, economic, and political divisions were in Marshall's time, they are even more pronounced today. Yet his message continues to be a forceful one for any of us who seek to build a sense of unity and shared purpose out of our diversity. Marshall believed in a type of civic solidarity that rested firmly on constitutional government and the rule of law, and his constitutional nationalism warrants the attention of all thoughtful citizens.

To date, what work has been done to tie Marshall to political theory has tended to consign him to conventional categories, with some seeing his thought as representative of the influence of the philosopher John Locke and the classical liberalism of the American founders, while others have described it as linked to classical versions of republicanism. Robert Faulkner, in an admirable study of Marshall's political thought, locates Marshall's emphasis on the protection of individual liberty and property rights squarely within the libertarian-Lockean framework, while Morton Frisch sees a nascent "constitutional republicanism" in Marshall's Supreme Court decisions.[16] Other Marshall scholars such as Richard Brisben have questioned the conceptual importance of either classical republicanism or liberalism as a means for appraising Marshall's thought, instead arguing that "[h]e was an individual whose values reflect the transition from republicanism to liberalism."[17] Among these scholars, Faulkner's work stands out as certainly the most detailed and extensive statement of Marshall's political thought. Acknowledging his work, we must certainly recognize Marshall's debt to the classical liberal tradition, with its emphasis on natural rights, private property, and a minimalist government.[18] But we must also try to reconcile this liberalism with the farsighted and at times even idealistic strand of nationalism that runs throughout his Supreme Court opinions. Motley were the qualities that made up John Marshall's thought, and the conventional labels only take us so far in describing its character. He believed that the United States needed a functioning government and common market, but he also thought that the stability of such goods relied on a healthy admiration, if not exaltation, of the nation's Constitution. By relegating this civic concern to the outer margins of Marshall's constitutionalism, we stop our ears to the complexity and strange harmonies of his philosophy.

So let us begin this search for understanding Marshall's thought with a resolve to move beyond political theory's familiar boxes. Marshall was not simply or only a liberal, conservative, or nationalist. He eludes easy categorization in his agreement and departures from these schools of thought. In fact, the plain black robe and somber trappings of the Supreme Court disguised a mind shaped by a variety of sources and traditions belonging to politics, law, and philosophy. Marshall's humble childhood, little formal education, and at times prosaic writing style should not deceive us about his intellectual acumen. Marshall was literate not only in the legal writings of Sir William Blackstone and Edward Coke but also in the Latin classics, including Homer, Horace, and Livy. He took no less delight in the Bible than he did in the works of Shakespeare, Edmund Burke, and Jane Austen.[19] These works fed an imagination that informed not only his jurisprudence, but also a broader vision of the role the Constitution might play in the new nation. His was a political theory that expanded beyond the court of law and the politics of the day to win the hearts and minds of all Americans.

The broader implications of Marshall's political thought are important not only for their historical import. As we will see, several concepts that are central to contemporary political thought—ideas of legitimacy, sovereignty, citizenship, and nationalism—were also of great interest to Marshall and were invoked in some of his most significant opinions. Debates concerning constitutional legitimacy familiar to the founding generation continue to be controversial, as seen in the writings of those such as Bruce Ackerman, David Strauss, and Ronald Dworkin.[20] Arguments related to national and state sovereignty remain highly charged in American politics, and prominent scholars of the founding such as Jack Greene, Forrest McDonald, and Alison LaCroix remain divided on the proper historical understanding of American federalism.[21] Similar debates have taken place concerning understandings of citizenship during the founding period. Scholars such as Joyce Appleby, John Diggins, and Michael Zuckert have emphasized notions of self-sufficiency, the exercise of natural rights, and commercial exchange as essential elements of citizenship in these years,[22] while authors such as Drew McCoy, Bernard Bailyn, and Lance Banning have discussed the centrality of republican themes of popular virtue, power, and political corruption.[23] Marshall's opinions address all of these controversies, and by adding his voice to these debates, we not only challenge historical interpretations of Marshall but also see how his thought intervenes in the political controversies of today.

Nor are the implications of Marshall's thought limited to the United States. The topic of nationalism, a concept by turns celebrate and derided, remains pivotal for scholars who stress the significance of national identity for understanding social and political loyalties.[24] Marshall was concerned with the acrimony generated by subnational allegiances, and he looked to the Constitution as playing a key role in unifying all Americans. Indeed, in his thought we find an early articulation and defense of principles similar to what the German philosopher Jürgen Habermas and others have called "constitutional patriotism," principles that emphasize the importance of the rule of law as embodied in a constitution as a form of civic identity for individuals in multicultural societies.[25] Yet the application of such ideas should not be limited to citizens in the developing world.[26] As national loyalties have taken on a new, at times troubling worldwide salience in the twenty-first century, it is worthwhile to revisit Marshall's constitutional nationalism for the lessons it imparts to theorists of nationalism today.

This book analyzes the development of Marshall's political thought as seen in several of his most important cases as Chief Justice, with his opinions in them providing a venue for explaining one of the core concepts of his political thought. Thus *Marbury v. Madison* illustrates Marshall's understanding of the basis of the Constitution's legal and political legitimacy, its moral authority as fundamental law. *McCulloch v. Maryland* sheds light on his view of constitutional sovereignty and the superiority of the law of the Constitution relative to national and state legislation. *Ogden v. Saunders* provides a venue for his understanding of the duties of citizenship and the meaning of liberty in the emerging commercial republic of the nineteenth century. And his opinions in the Native American Trilogy of *Johnson v. McIntosh* (1823), *Cherokee Nation v. Georgia* (1831), and *Worcester v. Georgia* (1832) bring to light his belief in a new form of American constitutional nationalism. Overall, these opinions go to the heart of Marshall's political thought: his belief in the Constitution's fundamental moral legitimacy, its purpose in mediating relations between the national government and the states, its promotion of a modern neo-republican form of liberty, and its institution of a nationalism extending beyond ethnic ties or the principles of liberal theory. Uniting these topics is Marshall's concern with explaining to citizens the Constitution's role in the still young republic, a role whose importance could not be understated as sectional conflicts threatened to tear the nation apart.

The first chapter focuses on the case of *Marbury v. Madison*, perhaps Marshall's most celebrated opinion. Although scholars have typically approached the opinion from the perspective of judicial review, this analysis views the case through the lens of constitutional legitimacy. The chapter argues that Marshall looked to a variety of familiar traditions to justify the binding authority of the Constitution, including the document's protection of rights, its representation of popular sovereignty, and its instrumental value in settling political questions. Moving beyond these themes, however, it argues that Marshall offers a unique theory of the Constitution's moral legitimacy that is derived from its embodiment of principles of good government and its status as the only viable legal order available to the nation. Hence, *Marbury* provides more than an argument on behalf of judicial supremacy and thus moves beyond the parameters of jurisprudential thinking alone. As we will see, the opinion adjudicates modern accounts of constitutional legitimacy while also illustrating Marshall's own theory of constitutional obedience.

Chapter 2 turns to *McCulloch v. Maryland*, drawing on Marshall's opinion in the case as well as a series of Virginia newspaper essays he penned anonymously in the aftermath of the Court's decision to explore his view of the Constitution's sovereignty. While scholars are typically divided on the question of whether *McCulloch* advocates national sovereignty or federalism, this chapter contends that Marshall rests ultimate sovereignty in neither the nation nor the states but in the Constitution itself. Moreover, his commitment to constitutional sovereignty is brought into sharper relief in his editorial exchanges with states' rights advocate Spencer Roane. The reasoning of the states rights' proponents troubled Marshall greatly, and he did not shy from insisting on its flaws. Writing as "A Friend of the Constitution," Marshall defends the Constitution as the final legal authority, superior to the political branches as well as the state governments. In this rare excursion into the realm of public opinion, Marshall set forth an understanding of sovereignty that was meant to nullify theories that would render the Constitution as a mere league between the states or identify its rule with a consolidated national government. By situating these essays alongside the Court's official opinion in *McCulloch*, one achieves a more comprehensive assessment of Marshall's understanding of the concept of sovereignty and the limits his idea imposed on national and state authority alike.

Chapter 3 examines Marshall's lone dissent as Chief Justice on a constitutional question in the case of *Ogden v. Saunders*. For Marshall, a seemingly innocuous New York bankruptcy act was a crisis point for a nation that was increasingly neglecting the law of the Constitution. While his fellow justices had upheld the act permitting state legislative interference in the terms of contracts governing default, Marshall argued that the legislation was not only incompatible with the Constitution's contract clause, but also undermined core aspects of the classical liberal and republican traditions that most Americans took for granted. But of even greater significance, Marshall's dissent also presents what can be seen as an early instance of what Philip Pettit would later term a "neo-republican" theory of nondomination that reconciled individual rights with the common good.[27] This fragile partnership of concepts was jeopardized by the prospect of arbitrary political power. Here the greatest threat posed by the act was not its disruption of the national economy, but the specter of state legislatures invading the liberties and private agreements reached by citizens. In *Ogden*, Marshall presents the Constitution as the only barrier against such invasions, and declares that it is among the powers of the Supreme Court to preserve the document's authority from future threats of legislative infraction interference. The dissent is significant in its defense of much of the political theory undergirding the Constitution, a theory including elements of classical liberalism and republicanism but also embracing a modern version of republican liberty that was possible only under the rule of law.

Chapter 4 considers some of Marshall's most controversial opinions, those comprising the so-called Native American trilogy. These opinions—*Johnson v. McIntosh*, *Cherokee Nation v. Georgia*, and *Worcester v. Georgia*—have rarely earned praise from Marshall scholars. Indeed, his role in these cases is often belittled, whether he is cast as an accessory to forced migration or a resigned and helpless witness to events beyond the Supreme Court's control. This chapter argues that such interpretations have neglected the broader contribution of Marshall's nationalism in these opinions, particularly his defense of the Constitution as an alternative source of national identification. In contrast to those who would frame nationalism in either narrow ethnic or universal liberal terms, Marshall offered an understanding of constitutional government broad enough to encompass all Americans. Although these cases revealed the institutional weaknesses of the judiciary, the opinions nevertheless show Marshall's understanding of the document's function in knitting together a people on the basis of shared principles concerning the rule of law.

Taken together, these cases point to a political theory that stood apart from the philosophical crosscurrents of his time. To be sure, there is much that is familiar in Marshall's political thought for the student of the founding era. Unsurprisingly in light of his Federalist Party credentials, Marshall was a vigorous defender of the sanctity of private property and economic rights generally, drawing heavily on "state of nature" theory and the classical liberal tradition. Yet in other instances, his emphasis on the importance of responsible citizenship and duty for securing individual liberty seemed more at home in ancient Greece and Rome than in the United States. In fact, Marshall drew on both liberal and republican themes in his opinions. Always wary of taking extreme positions, Marshall's moderation applied as much to his political philosophy as it did to his jurisprudence.

At the center of this political theory was Marshall's commitment to the Constitution as the foundation of America's legal and political life. An unabashed supporter of the Constitution in the Virginia Ratifying Convention, Marshall believed the Constitution was "the greatest improvement on human institutions." But the product of the framers could not rest content as a "splendid bauble" designed for admiration but possessing little practical value. Indeed, its instrumental function could not be exaggerated for a nation coping with its newfound responsibilities in the commercial and international arenas. For him, the document was principled and timeless, while also practical and flexible. As he famously put it, the Constitution was "intended to endure for ages to come, and, consequently, to be adapted to the various crises of human affairs." A government invested with "ample powers" to fulfill the prosperity and happiness of the nation required by extension "ample means for their execution." Thus Marshall was not only upholding the Constitution, but also explaining the rule of law to an audience still uncertain and in some cases skeptical of the new national government. With great purpose and effect, his words helped transfigure the Constitution from a written text into a kind of mythopoetic symbol, an abstract icon capable of compressing and evoking in a single word all of the complex history, negotiations, and laws that informed the nation.[28]

Citizens have and will continue to debate the fundamental questions of political theory raised in the cases explored here. Why do we continue to obey a Constitution over the course of several generations as opposed to some other legal convention or tradition? How much political authority should the national government possess? What obligations, if any, does citizenship entail? And just how do we define our national identity as Americans? Marshall's opinions addresses each of these disputes while pointing up a key question about the Constitution itself: to what extent can a written document generate national identity and unity in addition to its function in creating a legal order? Few would question Marshall's influence in his time. This book uncovers the lessons he imparts to our own.

1

John Marshall, *Marbury v. Madison*, and the Construction of Constitutional Legitimacy

Perhaps no other Supreme Court decision has offered a more lucid and forceful defense of the Constitution than *Marbury v. Madison* (1803). There are several explanations for the case's prominence in American legal history, including the Court's defense of the vested rights of individuals, its formulation of the "political questions" doctrine, and its assertion of judicial supremacy. For most scholars, the opinion's articulation of the principle of judicial review continues to loom particularly large.[1] All of these factors were indeed important in shaping the future course of the nation, and they are rightfully acknowledged in any assessment of the opinion's impact. But they do not tell the whole story. To enter into a discussion of *Marbury* is above all to enter into John Marshall's discussion of the fundamental authority of the Constitution. For in drafting the Court's unanimous opinion, Marshall did more than artfully avoid a clash between the Federalist judiciary and its Jeffersonian critics. More important, he offered a detailed justification of the binding authority of the Constitution, mapping out justifications familiar if still undeveloped at the time of the decision. In examining these theories as well as his own, *Marbury* yields a purchase for surveying the assumptions implicit in contemporary arguments concerning constitutional legitimacy.

Marshall's own theory of constitutional legitimacy runs deeper than the concepts and language familiar to most Americans of his day. At the heart of his theory is a belief in the Constitution's moral legitimacy, namely, its ability to provide fundamental law that, while perhaps not ideal, merits the respect and obedience of all citizens. Thus, while more familiar justifications based on rights, popular sovereignty, and the document's settlement function help orient his view of constitutional legitimacy, Marshall's theory of it includes at its center a subtle understanding of legitimacy inherent to the document itself. In justifying to his nineteenth-century audience his view of the Constitution's authority, we find the first evidence of Marshall's construction of a political theory that is distinctly his own, anchored neither to liberalism's emphasis on individual rights nor to a republican common good. Instead, as described in *Marbury*, Marshall's constitutional legitimacy is rooted in the fundamental importance of constitutional government, an earnest if optimistic belief he hoped his fellow citizens might one day share.

While *Marbury's* relevance for understanding the legal development of the United States needs little defense, scholars continue to disagree concerning the motives guiding Marshall's authorship of the Court's opinion. In light of the attitudes toward Marshall that we have already surveyed, it should come as little surprise that one's view of Marshall often corresponds to one's view of *Marbury*. The most widespread interpretation of the case casts him as a cunning political operator who wielded the Constitution as a weapon against opponents of the Federalist Party.[2] Almost as popular is the argument that he seized the occasion to achieve nonpartisan ends, specifically building the national influence of a weak Supreme Court that lacked the power to enforce its verdicts.[3] More recently, a small but emphatic camp of scholars has challenged the consensus opinion that *Marbury* was a self-interested product of either partisanship or institution building, arguing instead that the decision advanced a fair and neutral interpretation of the Constitution.[4] All of these readings, however, acknowledge the boldness of the decision, the finesse involved on Marshall's part, and the lasting impact of *Marbury* on American constitutional law. Thus Marshall's most hagiographic admirer could praise the opinion for its "perfectly calculated audacity" in engineering "a coup" on behalf of written constitutions "as bold in design and as daring in execution as that by which the Constitution had been framed."[5]

Absent among these evaluations, however, is a serious discussion of Marshall's role in establishing the Constitution's legitimacy. It is true that following its ratification, there was surprisingly little argument as to whether the American Constitution was the nation's supreme law. No "Anti-Constitution" Party ever took shape. Instead, its Antifederalist opponents swiftly turned from criticizing the Constitution's new national plan of government to effecting political change through its amendment process.[6] Most Americans acknowledged the Constitution as the binding law of the land, as both Federalists and Jeffersonians "accepted the Constitution as their standard," writes John Murrin, even as the two sides differed sharply on the question of how best to implement the government it created.[7] Moreover, as Keith Whittington has argued, despite Federalist fears of the so-called "Revolution of 1800" and the ascendency of Thomas Jefferson to the presidency, many Democratic-Republicans viewed their mission as rescuing the framers' work from the "constitutional errors" of their Federalist enemies.[8] Even so, the devil was in the details: loyalty to the Constitution meant different things to different people, so that long after its ratification, there was no consensus explanation for the Constitution's binding authority. The question not of *whether* but of *why* the Constitution was supreme law remained unsettled. To no small degree, Marshall's achievement in *Marbury* lay in his ability to sort through and lend a measure of coherence to these diverse explanations, thereby providing an opinion that organized and clarified the grounds for citizen's obedience to the Constitution.

Arguments concerning constitutional legitimacy remain alive and well. After all, governments must justify their existence to those who are required to live under them in any age.[9] Applied to political institutions such as Congress or the Supreme Court, questions concerning legitimacy typically address the right by which such institutions wield political authority over citizens.[10] In relation to constitutions, however, justifications of legitimacy must address an even more difficult question, which is why the words of the constitution should be followed as opposed to an alternative law, authority, or tradition.[11] Thus an ongoing conversation among scholars of European integration concerns the question of whether the legitimacy of traditional national constitutions can be made compatible with the legal strictures imposed by the supranational European Union. To answer this question, political thinkers led by Jürgen Habermas have struggled to find new justifications of constitutional authority that look to a constitution's function in knitting together people who lack a common heritage but share the same constitutionally governed territory.[12] Indeed, even in the United States, where constitutional legitimacy would now seem to be self-evident, the concept is much debated and surprisingly little understood. As a result, writes Richard Fallon, "confusion often results—not only among readers and listeners, but also . . . in the minds of those who write and speak about constitutional legitimacy."[13]

A survey of contemporary discussions of the Constitution's authority reveals that there is seldom any agreement concerning the one element of the Constitution that ensures its legitimacy. Some thinkers argue that the Constitution is a kind of benign straitjacket, an eighteenth-century text that protects individual liberties by constraining the ability of future elected officials and popular majorities to invade individual rights.[14] For these thinkers, the Constitution is delicate parchment: secure from the sullying touch of ordinary citizens, it issues its commands from under protective glass. Others contend that the Constitution is a continuing creation that binds citizens, at least for some duration of time, to the conditional consent given by the American people to its rule.[15] Their arguments suggest that the Constitution's actual appearance, frayed and worn, is the best one for a document that should sometimes be edited, marked through, and occasionally rewritten entirely. Finally, there are those who are persuaded that the Constitution binds citizens because of its instrumental role as a settlement device, providing a practical roadmap or set of "focal points" for organizing politics.[16] Proponents of this view conceive of the Constitution as a valuable but well-used atlas that continues to prove handy when the nation loses its way. Each of these justifications addresses important principles embodied in the American Constitution, and none of them discounts rights, consent, or the Constitution's instrumental value as sources of its legitimacy. Yet all too often these approaches look to a single paramount explanation that gives the Constitution its binding authority.[17] Today, as in Marshall's time, while there is virtually no debate among constitutional theorists as to whether the words of the Constitution bind judges and ordinary citizens alike to its rule, the question of why it is legitimate remains a subject of controversy.

The simplest way to provide a more unified approach to constitutional legitimacy would be to embrace each of these views, combining them into a more comprehensive defense of the Constitution's binding authority. Yet Marshall moved past these approaches to call attention to the Constitution's fundamental moral legitimacy. In doing so, he did not shrink from announcing his own admiration for the document, irrespective of its protection of rights, popular sovereignty, or the document's instrumental value. Important as these functions were, they were goods exterior to the Constitution itself. Marshall's loyalty ran deeper, grounding itself in the inherent benefits of the rule of law in and of itself. Nonetheless, he understood that his lofty fidelity to the document might not be shared by all Americans. To the best of this untrained attorney's ability, his theory of moral legitimacy is an effort in persuasion, crafted to prevail on the sympathies of the American people. A mix of high ideals and realistic appeals, it was an argument that in its complexity captured the fraught enterprise of convincing true believers and skeptics alike of the Constitution's legitimacy.

Marbury v. Madison Reconsidered

The facts of the case date back to the final days of the administration of President John Adams in March 1801. Worried that the incoming Jefferson administration and new Democratic-Republican Congress would fill the federal judiciary with party loyalists, Adams nominated a slate of fifty-two candidates to fill various federal judicial offices only days before leaving office.[18] Although the nominees were confirmed by the Senate and their written commissions signed by Adams, several commissions belonging to these "midnight judges" remained undelivered (the ultimate responsibility of then-Secretary of State John Marshall) when Thomas Jefferson was inaugurated as the nation's third President. On discovering the failed deliveries, Jefferson ordered his Attorney General, Levi Lincoln, to disregard Adams's appointments, basing his decision on the belief that non-lifetime appointments were revocable. After Jefferson sent his own candidates to the Senate for confirmation, a number of the previous appointees, including one William Marbury, petitioned the Supreme Court for a writ of mandamus ordering the new Secretary of State James Madison to recognize their commissions, along with those of the other Adams appointees.[19] Opening arguments in *Marbury v. Madison* began on February 10, 1803, with Attorney General Lincoln appearing on behalf of the government and former Attorney General Charles Lee representing Marbury.[20]

Notwithstanding able arguments presented by both attorneys, the verdict was unanimous. On February 24, Marshall delivered the Court's opinion, which was structured as a series of answers to three questions. First, did Marbury possess a title to his commission? Second, was the administration obliged to recognize his appointment? And finally, did the Supreme Court have the power to issue a writ of mandamus compelling the Secretary of State to recognize the commissions? Marshall concurred with the plaintiff's argument that Marbury did possess a proprietary right to his appointment and, furthermore, that the laws of the nation afforded him a legal remedy for the deprivation of his right. But in a surprising twist, the Chief Justice denied that the Supreme Court was the proper body for issuing a writ, holding that section 13 of the Judiciary Act of 1789, which in broadening the Supreme Court's jurisdictional authority had permitted the Court to hear *Marbury*, violated the constitutional provisions governing the Court's original jurisdiction prescribed in the Constitution. Thus the Court asserted the superiority of constitutional over ordinary law, striking down as invalid section 13, and with it, the legal standing of Marbury and the rest of Adams's outstanding appointees.

Marshall did not reserve his discussion of the Constitution to the rousing conclusion of *Marbury*. On the contrary, the Constitution is referenced eloquently and often provocatively throughout his opinion, and its authority is justified from multiple vantage points. Obviously, differences exist between Marshall's understanding of the Constitution's role and contemporary ones. But in allowing him to put forth his distinctive understanding of the Constitution's authority, *Marbury* provided Marshall with the opportunity to examine and apply what have become some of our most important theories of constitutional legitimacy. He began with a discussion of rights.

Marbury and the Protection of Rights

Among constitutional theorists, many argue that a written constitution's principal purpose is to secure citizens' rights.[21] For these thinkers, popular majorities, and particularly their elected representatives, are only too willing to override individual liberties if not legally restrained from doing so. Ronald Dworkin has made this case well over the course of several decades. "The constitutional theory on which our government rests is not a simple majoritarian theory," Dworkin writes. "The Constitution, and particularly the Bill of Rights, is designed to protect individual citizens and groups against certain decisions that a majority of citizens might want to make, even when that majority acts in what it takes to be the general or common interest."[22] Working from these assumptions, Dworkin has argued that a legitimate constitution must contain provisions that "disable" majority rule by codifying political and individual liberties alongside provisions that "enable" collective political decisions.[23] He goes on to assert that such a theory provides a constitutional conception of democracy that is based on the principle of equality rather than on its traditional association with majority rule. Accordingly, each member of the community is treated "with equal concern and respect," and citizens' most basic liberties are protected from infringement by the democratic process.[24] The argument is by no means a recent one: the purpose of the Constitution as a bridle on the dangers of popular rule was a prominent opinion voiced by political leaders throughout the founding era. One need only turn to the warnings of James Madison himself in his famous *Federalist #10* for evidence of this widespread concern with securing the "public good and private rights" from the special "danger" posed by majority or minority factions.[25]

Much of the first half of Marshall's opinion is centered on rights, and specifically on Marbury's right to assert legal title to his appointment as justice of the peace of the District of Columbia. Here it is important to note that it is unclear whether this matter needed to be addressed at all by the Court, let alone as its starting point. Indeed, Marshall's decision to pursue this question (as opposed to dismissing the case outright on jurisdictional grounds) has often cast suspicion on his motives in the case.[26] Nor was it clear that a discussion of rights belonged in the opinion at all. As John Brigham's discussion of *Marbury* points out, "It seems obvious now that this talk of rights is an appropriate form of inquiry, but 200 years ago the legal foundations of the national Union were anything but certain."[27] Perhaps it was partly out of concern for crafting such foundations that Marshall agreed with the prosecution's claim that Marbury did hold a title to his commission. As he put it, the key moment that guaranteed Marbury's title was not the formal delivery of the sealed commission or any other "solemnities" associated with the confirmation process (5 U.S. 160). Ceremonies of delivery were "directed by convenience, not by law." The key turning point was the president's signature, for once signed, deliberation had ceased, a decision had been rendered, and Adams's name had given immediate "force and effect to the commission" (5 U.S. 158). Thus inscribed, Adams's constitutional power of appointment was discharged completely: "his judgment" had been made, and "the right of the office" was conveyed in whole from the President to his appointee (5 U.S. 157). "The right to the office is *then* in the person appointed," concluded Marshall, "and he was the absolute, unconditional, power of accepting or rejecting it" (5 U.S. 162).[28]

Marshall drew on the familiar language of investiture to describe this transference. According to this doctrine, which had its origins in natural law philosophy, an individual was endowed with certain basic rights that were not subject to government control, including the possession and acquisition of private property.[29] On Marshall's understanding, Marbury was invested with a title to his office no different in its legal validity from "a patent for land" (5 U.S. 171). As was the case with any legal right, Marbury's was "protected by the laws of his country" (162). Marshall made the point in some of his most forceful and enduring language from the bench:

> The government of the United States has been emphatically termed a government of laws, & not of men. It will certainly cease to deserve this high appellation, if the laws furnish no remedy for the violation of a vested legal right (163).

Admittedly, Marbury's was a statutory, not a constitutional right. But for Marshall, Marbury's vested right was part of a bigger picture. Here he abstracted from the particular case of Marbury's commission to make the broader point that the protection of rights was a fundamental purpose of government. Marbury's right to his office "was not revocable," he averred, and was secured "by the laws of his country" (162). Indeed, he declared, "[t]he very essence of civil liberty" consisted of a citizen's legal protection from injury, and "one of the first duties of government" was to afford such protection (163). In making this argument, Marshall moved seamlessly from the case of William Marbury to discussing the Constitution's protection of vested statutory rights to an amplification of the document's defense of the "absolute rights of individuals" (171). Whatever tensions may have existed among these categories mattered less to him than the fact that individual rights had been endangered by the very government whose purpose was to secure them.

Having established Marbury's title to the commission, Marshall next turned to the question of whether the protection of this right was superseded by Jefferson's constitutional powers as Chief Executive. By addressing the topic, the Chief Justice implicitly repudiated the administration's position that the appointment process, along with executive branch decisions as a whole, was free from inspection by the judiciary. But he did not go so far as to claim that every decision made by the President and his officers was subject to review by the nation's courts, acknowledging a field of discretion within which the President exercised relatively free and independent power ("accountable only to his country in his political character, and to his own conscience") (5 U.S. 166). The exercise of this legitimate authority affected foremost "the nation, not individual rights, and, being entrusted to the Executive, the decision of the Executive is conclusive." These distinctly political powers adhering to the Office of the President entailed some measure of latitude by the Court, including the President's freedom to "appoint certain officers, who act by his authority and in conformity with his orders." The recent establishment by Congress of the Department of Foreign Affairs was an example ready at hand for Marshall. The officers of that department, Marshall explained, were "to conform precisely to the will of the president. He is the mere organ by whom that will is communicated." Indeed, as Marshall concluded with a tone of finality, "the acts of such an officer, as an officer, can never be examinable by the Courts."

Until this point in the opinion, the Jefferson administration appeared to be in the clear. Yet the Chief Justice next argued that the powers of the President did not extend to his ability to cancel Adams's appointments. Although the President and his cabinet possessed considerable authority for exercising their own discretion with respect to the affairs of the nation, particularly in foreign affairs, this area did not extend to the liberties of citizens. On occasions "where a specific duty is assigned by law, and individual rights depend on the performance of that duty," members of the executive branch complied with the Constitution rather than personal discretion (5 U.S. 166). In his capacity as a public minister of the law, Secretary of State Madison did not have the authority to refuse Adams's appointees and sport away vested rights—a minor distinction in the opinion that would prove to have far-reaching consequences for legal limitations on both presidential and judicial power.[30]

Recognizing Marbury's commission thus signaled a larger acknowledgment that the government of the United States rested its authority on its ability to safeguard rights from political interference, which in *Marbury* included the right of citizens to seek and obtain legal redress when those rights were violated. Accordingly, Marshall defended the constraining force of the rule of law against decisions of political leaders that conflicted with constitutional protections, even when leaders such as Jefferson drew support from popular majorities. But what authority stood behind these rights, codifying their protection in the form of a written constitution? Having established Marbury's legal rights, Marshall turned to the important role of the American people in the creation of the Constitution. His retelling of their performance of this task indicates how popular sovereignty complements traditional approaches to rights-based constitutionalism.

Marbury and the Role of Popular Sovereignty

A number of constitutional theorists look less to rights and more to the American people in locating legitimacy. The standard Lockean authorization of political consent—that is, as an express act of agreement to political authority by the governed—was one of the most familiar definitions of the concept in Marshall's time, and the significance of "majoritarian and populist mechanisms" as the keystone of the Constitution's legitimacy has continued to the present day.[31] Bruce Ackerman, for instance, describes the founding as a moment of revolutionary politics that entailed the development of "a distinctive form of constitutional practice" that "established paradigms for legitimate practices of higher lawmaking that subsequent generations have developed further."[32] Such moments of "higher lawmaking" are rare but monumentally important in American history, and possess certain characteristics: they attract public attention to a greater extent than the ordinary, everyday political process; they involve the voice of a mobilized opposition; and they entail a majority of the population's support for legal initiatives based on their merits.[33] Ackerman argues that these self-conscious exercises of popular sovereignty—specifically, at the time of the founding, Reconstruction, the New Deal, and the Civil Rights movements of the 1950s and 1960s—point up popular constitutive moments representing the "considered judgments made by the People," and the significance of such moments for constitutional government may even be weightier than those effected through the formal amendment process of Article V.[34] Like Dworkin, Ackerman celebrates the abstract principles found in the Constitution. Unlike Dworkin, however, he views these principles as levers for collective political action rather than justifications for an expansive conception of rights. As he put it in a recent summary of his position, "the Constitution's authority is generated by the mobilized and self-conscious commitments of We the People."[35]

Once he had established the Constitution's protection of rights, Marshall next turned to this issue of popular consent. The context of the discussion was whether the Supreme Court could exercise the discretion conferred on it by section 13 of the Judiciary Act of 1789, a provision that expanded the original jurisdiction of the Court marked out in Article III partly in an effort to relieve the heavy case burden on state courts (5 U.S. 174). For Marshall, the question of whether the Court could issue a writ of mandamus to Secretary Madison as permitted by Congress meant addressing the issue of "whether an act repugnant to the Constitution can become the law of the land," an issue he saw as "deeply interesting to the United States" (176).[36] To answer this question, Marshall without reservation invoked the will of the people and its authority in striking down section 13. As he saw it, the American people were the sole authority behind constitutional government, and the exercise of their power both authorized and narrowed the scope of future legislation. Taken in the abstract, Marshall stood on noncontroversial ground, the will of the people being one of many popular justifications of constitutional authority.[37] But here he was turning the argument back on the people's champion: Thomas Jefferson!

The reason that the Constitution was supreme to ordinary law, according to Marshall, was straightforward: the document's ultimate authority stemmed from the American people, who had both established and consented to its legal authority. Although Marshall does mention the intentions of the framers in *Marbury*, he emphasizes to a greater degree the role of the people as authors of the Constitution. Indeed, turning his opinion into what Kent Newmyer has called "a lesson in republican civics," he proceeded to claim that "the whole American fabric" was based on the principle that "the people have an original right to establish, for their future government, such principles as, in their opinion, shall most conduce to their own happiness" (5 U.S. 176).[38] The exercise of this right was an unusual exertion of the will of the people, one that could not and should not be repeated often. As he put it, the "original and supreme will" of the people had organized the government, allocating political powers among "different departments." In addition, the people did not grant authority to the three branches of government without qualification but had resolved to impose "limits not to be transcended by those departments." These limits apply especially to Congress: "The powers of the Legislature are defined, and limited; and that those limits may not be mistaken, or forgotten, the constitution is written." Both of these decisions—to form a national government and to set firm limits on its legislative authority—were based not on impulse but on the people's contemplation and decision to create a "fundamental and paramount law of the nation" (177). Only by understanding the popular origins of the Constitution could the reason for the binding character of its provisions—along with the invalidity of section 13—be fully apprehended.

Though most Americans acknowledged the concept of popular sovereignty, Marshall's specific focus of the Constitution's popular origins surely raised alarms among the opinion's Democratic-Republican readers, who had long feared that the Preamble's claim to speak on behalf of "We the People" aimed to collapse the thirteen state governments into a single, consolidated nation.[39] Marshall's portrayal of the Constitution as a product of collective deliberation and determination rendered by all Americans—or "reflection and choice," as Alexander Hamilton described it in *Federalist #1*—stood in direct contrast to notions that the document was nothing more than a transactional alliance among the sovereign states. But Marshall was hardly advocating mass democracy. While it was the people alone who were ultimately responsible for the momentous decision to create a Constitution, Marshall was careful not to exaggerate their future importance. Although the Constitution's supremacy was based on the principle of popular sovereignty, he cautioned that the collective exercise of this authority was reserved for exceptional occasions. Going forward, the American people would hold the narrower responsibility of holding elected officials liable for their political decisions largely at the ballot box.

Marshall's constitutionalism emphasizes the importance of popular sovereignty, agreeing with Ackerman on both the singularity of its exercise as well as the deliberation such movements require in order to confer legitimacy.[40] Moreover, as Marshall saw it, popular sovereignty was the ultimate source of the rights protections found in the Constitution. The authority of the people was "supreme," he declared in no uncertain terms, and because they could and did seldom exercise their authority, the principles they established were "designed to be permanent" (5 U.S. 176). Rights and consent were therefore two complementary pillars on which the Constitution's legitimacy stood. But do these two objects exhaust the justifications for constitutional obedience? What immediate, day-to-day guidance might the Constitution provide for national politics? While Marshall emphasized the Constitution's protection for rights and its basis in consent, he also located the source of the document's legitimacy in more functional terms. This understanding proved especially important in lending force to the closing argument of the Court's opinion.

Marbury and the Constitution as "Focal Point"

A third way that some constitutional theorists paint legitimacy is to portray the Constitution in more instrumental terms, by basing the text's binding authority on its ability to organize, settle, and otherwise provide safe direction to the political affairs of a nation. Beyond the document's status as a guardian of rights and product of consent, these thinkers rest its legitimacy on its ability to institute rules and maintain stability amid political disagreement.[41] Put simply, as the nation's supreme law, the Constitution furnishes "focal points" that act as a roadmap for the political system and legislative agenda. This function has been described best by legal theorist David Strauss, who supposes that individuals in any social setting unavoidably "disagree about various questions, large and small, related to how the government should be organized and operated."[42] Political directives that may seem straightforward and uncontroversial to many Americans, such as the appropriate duration of the President's term of office or whether Congress should have one or two chambers, might otherwise hamstring the political process and even lead to "disastrous" consequences for the stability of the state were they left open-ended. The Constitution prevents this scenario insofar as its textual provisions provide the guidance to "settle" a range of vital as well as seemingly innocuous political concerns. While the text may not offer an ideal solution to these fundamental political dilemmas, it does render a satisfactory one that most people can live with. Hence, says Strauss, obedience to the Constitution as supreme law is grounded in "the practical judgment that following this text, despite its shortcomings, is on balance a good thing to do because it resolves issues that have to be resolved one way or the other."[43] This approach shows that the Constitution is valuable not because it claims to enshrine either rights or the will of the people, but because it is a dispute-settlement mechanism, quieting interminable debates that have the potential to crowd out more productive deliberations. Put simply, constitutions are binding due to their practicality. Moreover, as Strauss argues, conceiving of the Constitution in this functional manner offers a clear and uncomplicated explanation for its status as supreme law, one that makes sense even to those with little attachment to the United States or even to the rule of law.[44]

Although the Constitution certainly settled a host of interstate difficulties that plagued the Articles of Confederation, this purpose had not achieved the same prominence as either rights or consent as an explanation for its authority at the time of *Marbury*. Indeed, as John Phillip Reid has pointed out, the great influence of the social contract tradition with its vocabulary of rights and consent often rendered alternative viewpoints of constitutional authority to a marginal status.[45] Moving beyond these two poles, Marshall's elevation of the provisions of the Constitution that gave order, rules, and direction to the nation's politics made clearer than ever before this instrumental function of the Constitution. Each part of the Constitution was intended to have a regulative effect on national politics, lest any of its clauses should be rendered as "mere surplusage" and "form without substance" (5 U.S. 174). In arguing these points, Marshall set aside the familiar language of rights and consent and drew attention to the organizational role the Constitution would play in American politics.

One national focal point that figures heavily in *Marbury* is the Supreme Court itself. At the time of *Marbury*, the Constitution lacked an authoritative and final expositor, and it was by no means clear that the Court could pass judgment on the constitutionality of the actions of the political branches.[46] Yet Marshall is emphatic that that such judgment was indeed the prime responsibility of the Court, if not its exclusive province. Marshall expressed no doubts here. Turning to the language of Article III, he notes that the Constitution "vests the whole judicial power of the United States" in a single Supreme Court and "such inferior courts" established from time to time by Congress (5 U.S. 173).[47] Its words, he wrote, "expressly extended" this power "to all cases arising under the laws of the United States." It was thus the Supreme Court's "province and duty . . . to say what the law is" when a statute appeared to conflict with the Constitution (177). It was up to the Court, in other words, to evaluate legislation, and even its own conduct, against the standards erected by the Constitution. Moreover, he continued in a flourish of legal positivism, the Court did not reach its decisions on the basis of extraneous legal traditions or particular ideologies. Instead, the object that governed judges' conduct in their official character was the constitutional text itself, given that the framers had "contemplated that instrument as a rule for the government of courts, as well as the legislature" (180). Thus the Court's decisions on constitutional questions were determined solely by the Constitution, and as a rulebook for the nation and the nation's courts, it was a document that must necessarily be opened, read, "looked into," and "inspected" (179, 180). The verdicts of the Court would be governed by no ancillary authority, legal or otherwise.

In addition to providing guidance for its interpretation, the Constitution furnished specific signposts to define and limit congressional power. For example, Article I prohibited state-issued paper money. It also expressly forbade ex post facto laws and bills of attainder. Article III provided clear instructions to the judiciary regarding treason convictions. Quoting this clause in full, Marshall notes that "no person shall be convicted of treason unless on the testimony of two witnesses to the same overt act, or on confession in open court" (5 U.S. 179). Emphasizing that "many other selections" might be mentioned, he went on to affirm that such provisions illustrated that the Constitution was a guiding "rule" for both legislative and judicial decisions, and that such "constitutional principles" must never yield to an act of Congress (179–80). Reducing the Constitution to a status equal to that of "any ordinary act of the Legislature," he warned, would give "to the Legislature a practical and real omnipotence" in the nation's political affairs (178).

Finally, Marshall draws attention to the oath of office as a constitutional focal point common to all branches of government insofar as it puts all members of the government under the obligation to support and defend the Constitution. Approaching the close of his decision, he portrays this oath not as an empty ceremony, but as a solemn vow to subordinate all decisions and "conduct in their official character" to the strictures of constitutional law (5 U.S. 180). Why else, he asks, must a judge take this oath "to discharge his duties agreeably to the Constitution of the United States if that Constitution forms no rule for his government?" If the oath did not carry with it the duty to regard the Constitution as such a rule, then both prescribing and taking the oath would be "equally a crime." Although the oaths taken by presidents, justices, and members of Congress upon assuming office were different in length and content, in Marshall's eyes they were uniform insofar as they obligated all to uphold the Constitution. Thus, as he puts it in the dramatic conclusion to *Marbury*, the "particular phraseology of the Constitution of the United States" confirms the document's superiority to legislative law, and that "courts, as well as other departments, are bound by that instrument."

In the short term, the Court's decision in *Marbury* proved uncontroversial, as the opinion met with little public outcry.[48] The silence, however, was temporary. The Jeffersonians soon drew battle lines against the Marshall Court, perceiving it as the last Federalist stronghold in the national government.[49] In 1804, a warning shot was fired in the Chief Justice's direction when Jefferson's followers in the House of Representatives impeached Justice Samuel Chase. Though Chase was not convicted, the message to Marshall was clear. As for Jefferson himself, his personal animus toward the Court in general and Marshall in particular never ebbed, even after his presidency ended. Writing in 1819 to Judge Spencer Roane of the Virginia Court of Appeals—whom we will meet again in short order—the former president repudiated the notion that an unelected Supreme Court possessed "the right to prescribe rules" governing Congress and the president. Giving the judiciary such absolute authority over the Constitution's interpretation would reduce the document to "a mere thing of wax," he wrote, which justices "may twist and shape into any form they please."[50] In hindsight, *Marbury* represented the first episode in a long and often acrimonious clash between the Court and its Jeffersonian critics.

Yet *Marbury*'s failure to quell partisan rancor should not diminish Marshall's attempts at conciliation. As Gordon Wood points out, *Marbury* was the only occasion during Marshall's long tenure as Chief Justice that the Court declared an act of Congress unconstitutional, and Marshall's statement of the Court's role in the American constitutional system attempted to strike a note of restraint.[51] In justifying the binding authority the Constitution exercised on citizens, Marshall mostly drew on familiar concepts, not innovative ones. The Constitution protected the rights of citizens. It was authorized if not written by the original and supreme will of the people. While securing rights and embodying consent, it also served as a practical rulebook, identifying the Supreme Court as the major site of constitutional interpretation while imposing boundaries on the reach of the national government. Among other matters, these boundaries included the limitations the Constitution placed on the political powers of the President and the ability of Congress to extend the Supreme Court's jurisdiction beyond constitutional limits. In *Marbury*, each of the dominant explanations for the Constitution's legitimacy—rights, consent, and focal points—are parts in a broader and more unified story about its authoritative role in the United States.

But if each of these approaches to legitimacy furnishes only a partial understanding of the Constitution's role in the United States, does merely lumping them together create a greater attachment to that document? Does creating such a partnership of principles add to or strengthen the Constitution's legitimacy, or does it merely reinforce existing reasons for obedience? In response to these questions, it is worth paying attention to still other ways in which Marshall describes the Constitution in *Marbury*, and how in doing so he points to a theory of the Constitution's moral legitimacy that refers to but also transcends the arguments examined so far.

Marshall's Theory of Constitutional Legitimacy

For many contemporary political and legal theorists, constitutions derive their legitimacy from more than their protection of liberties, their representation of consent, or their instrumental role in providing institutional and legal focal points. These theories require a more aspirational justification, linking a constitution's legitimacy to its ability to provide a just legal regime based on its moral justifiability or its worthiness of respect. In the words of Habermas, "legitimacy means that there are good arguments for a political order's claim to be recognized as right and just."[52] Disagreement abounds, however, concerning what threshold regimes must meet to attain this moral legitimacy. Ideal theories of moral legitimacy depressingly conclude that while no constitution is fully legitimate, one can nonetheless be binding to the extent that it approximates an ideal moral standard such as justice or equality.[53] For instance, Sotirios Barber and James Fleming have defended a moral or "philosophic" approach to constitutional interpretation, emphasizing the "abstract moral and political principles" embodied in the Constitution that demand from justices "normative judgments about how [such principles] are best understood, not merely historical research to discover relatively specific original meanings."[54] Such arguments see legitimacy in idealistic terms only, insofar as they supply a model or set of values that a constitution may approximate but never fully realize.[55] Alternatively, minimal theories of moral legitimacy insist that it is not necessary for a constitution to be morally legitimate in absolute terms in order to bind citizens to its rule, especially if a better, alternative constitutional order cannot be realized swiftly and peacefully.[56] Indeed, as Richard Fallon claims, a "sufficiently just" constitution is better than no constitution at all, and so a constitution's fundamental legitimacy may arise simply "from the facts that it exists, that it is accepted as law, that it is *reasonably* (rather than completely) just, and that agreement to a better constitution would be difficult if not impossible to achieve."[57] Joseph Raz takes the argument a step further, reasoning that "*as long as they remain within the boundaries set by moral principles*, constitutions are self-validating in that their validity derives from nothing more than the fact that they are there."[58] But whether these approaches emphasize an ideal or minimal moral legitimacy, they are in agreement that a constitution derives its legitimacy not only from rights, consent, or its settling function alone, but also from its ability to situate these principles within the parameters of its broadly or narrowly defined moral justifiability.

In *Marbury*, Marshall is sensitive to both of these understandings of a constitution's moral legitimacy. For his own part, Marshall consistently extolled the virtues of the Constitution and the political regime it created: he is not called the "defender of the Constitution" without reason.[59] Yet he was also aware that a more commonsensical defense of the Constitution's merits was required to drive home to readers the practical benefits of the document's supremacy. As a result, Marshall's theory of moral legitimacy relies on two modes of persuasion. On the one hand, he draws attention to the Constitution's embodiment of principles that facilitate good and stable government. On the other hand, he emphasizes the necessity of the rule of law for any government at all. The Constitution, in *Marbury's* more sober moments, was if nothing else a law the nation could not do without. By turns idealistic and realistic, Marshall's full-fledged devotion to the Constitution was tailored to his awareness of the obstacles and skepticism any new legal order encounters in the court of public opinion.

We see in *Marbury* this resistance toward making a stark choice between ideal and minimalist theories, with Marshall drawing on both approaches to advance a different, more moderate concept of moral legitimacy. On the one hand, his rhetoric in referring to constitutional principles is far too muscular for the comparatively uninspiring minimalist theories. On the other hand, he never describes the Constitution as ideal, nor did he hesitate to point out that government under the Constitution is better than no government whatsoever.[60] Marshall's moral legitimacy falls below standards that could never be realistically met but above those that any legal regime might possess. Thus, in contrast to approaches that set the bar of moral legitimacy either too high or too low, *Marbury* stakes out a middle ground.

Marshall's personal devotion to the Constitution can hardly be overstated. Throughout his Supreme Court opinions, he never failed to refer to the document in the most favorable, even praiseworthy terms. If it was not perfect law, it was as close to perfection as could be expected from human hands. The Constitution, as he saw it, supplied all the qualities one would hope to find in a just political regime: equality before the law, clear and coherent procedures, and institutions conducive to the public good. On his account, the Constitution needed no auxiliary justification for its legitimacy. Pure and simple, the Constitution was binding because it was good law, a belief Marshall did not shy away from declaring in strong terms. Indeed, for Marshall, the Constitution demanded a form of devotion that verged on the reverential. As Chief Justice, he often spoke of the document in religious terms, invoking it as the nation's "sacred" law.[61] Nor did he avoid such language in *Marbury*. He minced no words when declaring that the oath taken by political officers to support the Constitution is an ethical as well as a legal bond: "How immoral," he exclaims, "to impose [an oath] on them, if they were to be used as the instruments, and the knowing instruments, for violating what they swear to support!" (5 U.S. 180).

Elsewhere in the opinion he again applies similar rhetoric when asserting that the Constitution is worthy of the same veneration Americans attached to their state constitutions, which had long "been viewed with so much reverence" (178).[62] Marshall was ever mindful of this moral dimension of the rule of law, one that could not be adequately captured in legal terms alone. Indeed, in Marshall's personal estimate, the document possessed a quality that bordered on the sacred.

Yet such devotional rhetoric, no matter how moving, has its limits. Marshall knew his argument needed something more than a stock of literary flourishes, and so he emphasized to his readers the principles embraced within the Constitution and its framing. Similar to ideal theories of moral legitimacy that emphasize ideas such as justice, consent, and equality, Marshall's rhetoric is anchored to the Constitution's embodiment of fundamental principles that distinguished it from other legal documents. Referring to the constitutive power of the people, Marshall describes their accomplishment not only as an instantiation of the people's consent, but also as the express pronouncement of "such principles as, in their opinion, shall most conduce to their own happiness" (5 U.S. 176). Having been declared, these principles are "deemed fundamental" and become "permanent," in large part because of the time and effort involved in their pronouncement. Inscribed in the Constitution, they are "the basis on which the whole American fabric has been erected." Although Marshall does not specify these principles in detail, they can be easily deduced from his opinion: the formation of a national government, the defined and limited powers of the legislative branch, the Constitution's protection of civil liberties, and its supremacy to legislative acts, as well as specific, legal directives based on common law and earlier legal traditions (163, 176–77, 179). Together, these "essential" principles and rules supply the bedrock for the rule of law, while also entailing a duty on the part of public officials to regard them as binding upon their conduct (180). Hence it was necessity and "the very essence of judicial duty," Marshall wrote, that obligated the Court in some cases to examine the legality of statutes that were said to conflict with the constitutional text (178). While consent did play a legitimizing force for Marshall, it was the institution of those principles conducive to good government and the people's happiness that helped make written constitutions "the greatest improvement on political institutions." In short, it was not the act of consent in and of itself that was important for the Constitution's legitimacy, but the principles and objects that the people consented to and helped create.

Surely Marshall did not expect all Americans to share his level of esteem for the Constitution. He had some more convincing to do. Take away the august characters of supporters such as Madison, Hamilton, and Washington, and it was unlikely the document's "intrinsic merits" would ever have secured its ratification, he once admitted.[63] For these reasons, *Marbury* invokes justifications that might be more acceptable to a broader range of Americans: ideas of popular sovereignty, rights, and its instrumental functions, but also the notion that the Constitution derived legitimacy from its status as the nation's fundamental law in the absence of better alternatives. Nor was this a mere philosophical thought experiment. The argument reminded readers, however indirectly, of the travails of the country under the Articles of Confederation. Here he provides a hint of what might follow from rejecting its legitimacy, producing for his readers a pair of stark political alternatives from which they must choose.[64] The options typically appear overdrawn, perhaps intentionally, and they are posed to a variety of people, including judges, legislators, and the general public. Judges are obliged to follow and defend the Constitution as "paramount law," or they are "reduced to the necessity of" ignoring its words entirely, so that in effect they "close their eyes on the Constitution, and see only the law" (5 U.S. 179). Again, when political officers swear to uphold and defend the Constitution, the oath of office either forms "a rule for the government of courts, as well as of the Legislatures," or else its administration is a crime "worse than solemn mockery" (180). Either an act of Congress contrary to the Constitutions must be struck down, or the "legislature may alter the Constitution by an ordinary act," making written constitutions "absurd attempts on the part of the people to limit a power in its own nature illimitable" (177). Finally, *Marbury* declares in bold and sweeping terms that "no middle ground" exists on the question of whether the Constitution is "a superior, paramount law, unchangeable by ordinary means," or "on a level with ordinary legislative acts, and, like other acts, is alterable when the legislature shall please." For Marshall, one either accepts the Constitution as furnishing a legal order capable of holding the nation together, or one is confronted with an unlimited and potentially tyrannical legislature.

Yet presenting the Constitution's moral legitimacy as a weave of principles and pragmatism was not enough for Marshall. Throughout the course of *Marbury*, he endeavors to amplify the Constitution's legitimacy by stressing its foundational and even self-assertive character. Repeatedly he depicts the Constitution as exercising its own power, investing authority in the judiciary, prescribing rules governing admissible evidence, and constraining officers of the national government (5 U.S. 173, 179, 180). At times he stands aside, allowing the Constitution to speak for itself, as when he carefully notes that it is the Constitution and not the Supreme Court that "has declared" where "their jurisdiction shall be original" and "where it shall be appellate" (174). Every word of the document is important for the nation, Marshall belabors, for "it cannot be presumed that any clause in the Constitution is intended to be without effect." The Constitution thus exerted an agency and power that distinguishes it from the Articles of Confederation. Moreover, he makes it clear that denying its legitimacy would lead to more than legal confusion or policy gridlock. Of worse consequence, it would render the founding "entirely void," "subvert the very foundation of all written constitutions," and undermine all the "principles and theory of our government" (178). Marshall's theory of the Constitution's moral legitimacy is one with teeth: in *Marbury*, the American Constitution—the entire American Constitution—is given its own voice as the nation's supreme law.

Marbury v. Madison, like most of Marshall's Supreme Court opinions, is a portrait of concise and methodical writing. It therefore appears odd, in light of his characteristic economy of words, that the language he uses to describe the Constitution requires more elaboration than he provides. How may we finally characterize Marshall's theory of constitutional legitimacy? *Marbury* indicates that the Constitution encompassed more than a bundle of ideas about rights, consent, and settlement functions. Constitutional loyalty ran deeper than that for Marshall, and it is on this subject that we first really enter into his political theory. He viewed the document as legitimate because as the nation's supreme law it embodied principles citizens might not simply defer to but also revere as just foundations for good and stable government. Yet he recognized that for the time being such public regard was not in the offing, and so rested moral legitimacy on lower but more solid ground. As he argued in practical if not inspiring terms, the federal Constitution was the only one the nation had. In the absence of realistically attainable alternatives, and in light of the dysfunction that plagued the nation under the Articles, its importance for supplying a coherent system of law applicable to all citizens should not be taken lightly. Marshall's personal view was that the Constitution deserved the veneration of all citizens as good law. But, recognizing the distance between his views and those of his fellow citizens, between his political ideals and circumstances as they stood, he held that the Constitution's moral legitimacy also stemmed from the fact that the nation could simply not do without one.

Conclusions

Marbury stands as both an invitation and a provocation to contemporary debates concerning constitutional legitimacy. Marshall's constitutionalism runs counter to approaches such as those of Dworkin, Ackerman, and Strauss, which tend to concentrate on distinctive purposes or functions as conferring legitimacy. Among these purposes are its protection of individual liberties, enshrinement of popular consent, and establishment of a blueprint for organizing politics. Because Marshall does not base his theory of legitimacy on any exclusive justification, his opinion fosters a common ground for contemporary conversation concerning the basis of constitutional legitimacy. Yet, however crucial these functions of the Constitution are to justifying its legitimacy, they do not fully capture Marshall's comprehensive understanding of its authority. Marshall envelops these attributes in his constitutionalism, but also develops the argument that the Constitution embodies a fundamental moral legitimacy that elevates the standing of the document in the hearts and minds of citizens. Neither utopian dreamer nor hardboiled realist, he conceived of the Constitution as simultaneously principled and practical, embracing both the philosophical ends and the practical means required to establish a just and workable regime. He turns to both of these dimensions of moral legitimacy in *Marbury*, declaring his admiration for the document as well as the more mundane necessity of its role in American government. Thus *Marbury* offers a concept of constitutional legitimacy that acknowledges but moves beyond contemporary conceptualizations, forcing us to wonder if obedience to the Constitution must in some measure rest within the document itself, regardless of whatever external functions it exercises. For Marshall, a more intrinsic, self-referential justification of the Constitution's legitimacy deserved notice in addition to rights, popular sovereignty, and focal points. To simplify his view only marginally, the Constitution bound citizens because it was a good Constitution. As we will see in the chapters that follow, it was a point he returned to frequently during his tenure on the Supreme Court.

In setting forth Marshall's theory of constitutional legitimacy, *Marbury* also illustrates how constitutional loyalty is not simply a given, but must be constructed and is frequently contested. The opinion in *Marbury* is an example of how the Constitution's legitimacy was and indeed remains a formed conviction rather than an automatic one, the achievement of political craftsmanship as much as a product of the power of its words alone. Nor was Marshall unaware of the importance of his words within the larger political context of his time. As Christopher Eisgruber has argued, in light of the general public's largely ambiguous attitude toward the national government during his tenure, the Chief Justice's rhetoric was directed toward convincing Americans "that national institutions, including the federal judiciary, would govern well."[65] This effort is particularly visible in his showdown with the Jefferson administration.

Revisiting *Marbury* requires readers to reconsider the opinion and the conventional wisdom that it is primarily concerned with judicial review. It also requires us for the first time to reconsider the conventional wisdom on John Marshall, whose careful political theorizing is on display in his concern with the concept of constitutional legitimacy. That said, *Marbury* and Marshall do not provide the final word on the topic of legitimacy. It is abundantly clear that Americans will continue to define and debate their constitutional fidelity according to many different standards. For Marshall, the tensions between these understandings should not necessarily be a source of worry.[66] Rather, his arguments in *Marbury* show that the justifications we give for the Constitution's legitimacy cannot neglect the general acknowledgment that it is supreme law—a requirement that applies to presidents, legislators, judges, and ordinary citizens alike.

Concerning the legitimacy of the laws of the national government, however, Marshall still had some convincing to do. Dodging a showdown with Jefferson—and a very real prospect of impeachment by the Republican Congress—did not put an end to animosity directed toward the judiciary and the national government. As he would soon learn, fears and resentment toward centralized power ran deep and had not died with the American Revolution. The backlash his Court would encounter in the aftermath of his decision in the case of *McCulloch v. Maryland* (1819) would demonstrate the extent of Marshall's challenge in establishing the Constitution's sovereignty.

2

John Marshall,
McCulloch v. Maryland, and the
Concept of Constitutional Sovereignty

A s important as the Constitution's moral legitimacy was to John Marshall in *Marbury*, the document's supervision of state and national
policy was equally important to his vision of the broader national role of
the Constitution. His opinion in the case of *McCulloch v. Maryland* (1819),
while engaging in a lively debate on nationalism and federalism, was also
the testing ground for his idea of constitutional sovereignty. Indeed, in
the opinion and its aftermath, Marshall took up a question that political
theorists of every stripe must at some point address: what person, body, or
law should be the highest authority or power in society? As in *Marbury*,
Marshall again found himself ensnared in a partisan fight, on this occasion with the states' rights activists in his home state of Virginia instead
of Thomas Jefferson. This time, however, Marshall's argument on behalf
of constitutional sovereignty spilled outside the courtroom and into the
pages of the nation's newspapers.

Like legitimacy, sovereignty has long been a contested idea in the
American political order. In coming to terms with the character of a central
government, many Americans throughout the founding era argued the
philosophical question of whether sovereignty could be divided or not.
Many more addressed the practical implications of this debate, locating
ultimate sovereignty in either the federal government or among the states.
In *McCulloch*, Marshall is a participant in these arguments, investing sovereignty in both the states and the national government. Yet sovereignty

meant more to Marshall than its service as an expedient to quiet discord about his opinion. Nor was it a purely legal concept. Both in the opinion and its immediate aftermath, Marshall pointed to the Constitution as exercising the highest sovereignty in the United States, standing above and keeping watch over the rough-and-tumble political process.

Marshall was again confronted with a topic that, while a touchstone of American political vocabulary, often caused Americans to speak past each another. Indeed, sovereignty was a subject that few thinkers surveying the new political landscape could cogently articulate. As Christian Fritz recently put it, following the Revolution, "few disputed that the people would rule as the sovereign speaking through written constitutions. But in putting this idea into practice, Americans parted company with one another."[1] Even at the time of the Constitution's ratification, Walter Bennett contends, the "nature and location of sovereignty" remained a concept "so elusive" that any argument making use of the term could be made to appear insufficient if not outright wrong.[2] In fact, the site of sovereignty remained open to debate well into the early nineteenth century.[3] Indeed, as Hugh Willis describes, the Constitution's status as representing the sovereign authority of the American people was a concept that took root in public opinion only gradually, over the course of "long years of constitutional history and profound opinions of the United States Supreme Court."[4]

Enter Marshall. As a public figure, he was well situated to play a significant role in arguments concerning the character of sovereignty. Yet examinations of Marshall's understanding of the concept in McCulloch have gone largely unnoticed. Most students of the opinion have viewed it as an unambiguous defense of the powers of the national government, pointing to Marshall's support for a broad interpretation of the Constitution's words and his characterization of the document's creation by the American people rather than the states.[5] Some, however, have taken a more tempered view of McCulloch, contending that Marshall defended a notion of national power that reserved a significant amount of authority for the states.[6] For example, a more state-centered view of the opinion has been recently advanced by Sotirios Barber, who has argued that McCulloch charted a "constitutional federalism" that represented a middle ground between complete state sovereignty and an extreme nationalism that denied any limits on Congress' authority.[7] But while these interpretations arrive at different conclusions regarding the scope of Marshall's nationalism and federalism, they have one thing in common: a tendency to relegate Marshall's theory of constitutional sovereignty to the periphery.

The neglect of Marshall's constitutional theory in *McCulloch* is not the only omission that characterizes many analyses of the case. Although examinations of *McCulloch* typically begin and end with the opinion itself, this focus can tell one only so much. A full reckoning of *McCulloch*, and especially Marshall's political thought, must involve his rare public commentary on the case. In the summer of 1819, Marshall articulated a defense of his *McCulloch* opinion in the popular press, the sole occasion in his long career of public service when he would engage in a journalistic discussion of any judicial decision.[8] Writing pseudonymously in a number of Virginia newspapers, he expanded on the Court's opinion, defending it against the attacks of critics. Although these essays have been acknowledged by scholars as providing a more wide-ranging defense of Marshall's decision, their importance has been considerably undervalued. For the essays provide more than a mere defense or rationalization of *McCulloch* and consist of far more than partisan bickering. Instead, they go further to offer a full-fledged argument on behalf of Marshall's concept of constitutional sovereignty.

McCulloch v. Maryland Revisited

The economically tumultuous years of the late eighteenth century provided the backdrop for *McCulloch*.[9] When the twenty-year charter of the First Bank of the United States expired in 1811, the Republican Congress, which had always looked askance at the national bank for its centralizing tendencies, successfully blocked its renewal. But the financial strain of the War of 1812 reminded the nation of the need for a streamlined economic system, and the Bank was rechartered in 1816 amid a wave of postwar nationalist euphoria. Upon its renewal, the Bank immediately began opening local branches throughout the country, ignoring objections raised by both private and state-chartered institutions that anticipated a significant loss of business to the national branches. Such fears were soon realized: the Bank flourished as the nation's major source of credit, and the backing of the federal government gave its branches a decided competitive advantage over their local counterparts. Within three years of its reincorporation, the Bank enjoyed widespread acclaim as a leading driver behind the nation's postwar economic boom.

By late 1818, however, Americans had largely soured on the Bank. Many branches were forced to recall loans at a rapid rate to offset a drop in American commodity prices overseas, an action that jolted local economies. Additionally, instances of embezzlement, fraud, and general mismanagement by branch officials that often went ignored or unpunished by federal authorities further heightened local resentments.[10] The response by elected officials was swift. By 1819, several state legislatures had passed laws that attempted to chip away at the Bank's financial influence within their respective states. Among these was Maryland, which targeted the Bank by imposing a banknote tax or an annual $15,000 fee on the operations of all banks without a state charter. The cashier of the Baltimore branch of the Second Bank of the United States, James McCulloch, refused to pay either sum to the state, which prompted Maryland to file suit against the Second Bank. After a Baltimore county court and the state Court of Appeals upheld the Maryland law, the case was appealed to the Supreme Court on the basis of a writ of error filed by the Bank.

The Supreme Court soon sensed the gravity of the confrontation between state and national government, extending the duration of oral arguments to one week while allowing both the prosecution and defense an additional lawyer. Adding to public interest in the case was the impressive roster of attorneys. Congressman Joseph Hopkinson, U.S. Attorney for the District of Columbia Walter Jones, and state Attorney General Luther Martin would defend the state of Maryland, while U.S. Attorney General William Wirt, future Attorney General William Pinkney, and a young Daniel Webster represented the Second Bank. The courtroom was packed when the first of nine days of arguments began on February 22, 1818. The issues raised in the trial were hardly novel, but they were argued passionately and in detail: counsel for Maryland defended a strict construction of the Constitution that emphasized the right of the state to tax the branch, while attorneys for the Bank focused on the institution's legitimacy by pointing to Congress' implied powers as granted by the Constitution.

Marshall delivered the unanimous opinion of the Court on March 6, 1819, a mere three days after the trial's closing arguments.[11] The opinion raised and responded to two key questions. First, was Congress empowered to charter a national bank? And second, granting the constitutionality of the Second Bank, could Maryland levy a tax on one of its state branches "without violating the Constitution"? (17 U.S. 401, 425). Writing for the Court in what proved to be one of his lengthiest opinions as chief justice, Marshall carefully parsed both questions, confirming that the Bank's incorporation was constitutional based on "a fair construction" of the Constitution and the implied powers of Congress (406).[12] Next, he found that Maryland was prohibited from imposing any tax on a branch's operation. While states did exercise taxation power concurrently with the national government, that authority did not allow Maryland, or any other state government, to interfere with the policies of the national government pursuant to the Constitution. Hence, he concluded with respect to the state's bank tax, "such a tax must be unconstitutional" (437).

Public reaction to the *McCulloch* decision varied widely by region. In the industrial North, where the Second Bank remained popular and the effects of the economic recession were milder, newspapers cast the Supreme Court's decision in a favorable light, while in the South and West, editorials were more mixed in their tone. But in Marshall's home state of Virginia, opposition to the ruling was fierce and ran deep. Marshall, a local boy, had long been detested by powerful Democratic-Republicans in Richmond—the "Richmond Junto," as they came to be known—who stoked anger against *McCulloch* as the latest blow to Virginian sovereignty.[13] The Junto's chief complaint was not so much that *McCulloch* had declared the Second Bank constitutional, but that its doctrine of Congress' implied powers (and especially Marshall's reading of the necessary and proper clause) would render the states wholly subordinate to the political will of the national government.[14] A closer look at Marshall's opinion in the case shows that the ferocious criticism of its detractors was not entirely without merit.

McCulloch on National Sovereignty

Sovereignty has long been understood to imply the presence of a single, ultimate political authority as one of its necessary attributes. It was certainly the widespread association of sovereignty with notions of omnipotence and unity that such luminaries as Thomas Hobbes, Jean Bodin, and Hugo Grotius contemplated when formulating their distinct understandings of sovereign power as the unitary and indivisible promulgation of law. Similar concepts of indivisible sovereignty remained commonplace in the Anglo-American world of the eighteenth century.[15] Indeed, as Gordon Wood has described, even into the 1770s, the belief in a supreme and absolute authority as a necessary attribute of government was taken for granted by most thinkers.[16] Admittedly, by the time of the American Revolution, some had begun to articulate a coherent concept of divided sovereignty. But even as late as 1787, as Forrest McDonald has shown, the concept remained ill defined. Indeed, however much the new Constitution's federal structure in practice belied the abstract principle, a stubborn belief persisted throughout the early years of the republic that any state must possess an ultimate site of political sovereignty. As McDonald puts it, those colonists "who thought about the matter accepted the indivisibility of sovereignty as an abstract theoretical proposition," even as local politics was increasingly being organized along the lines of "a *de facto* system of divided sovereignty."[17]

At first blush, *McCulloch* seems to offer an unequivocal defense of this principle. The clearest evidence appears in Marshall's rejection of the many arguments made by the attorneys for Maryland on behalf of state sovereignty. During the trial, counsel for Maryland had insisted at length that the Constitution emanated not from the American people but from "the act of sovereign and independent States" (17 U.S. 402). Accordingly, the powers of the national government were seen as subordinate to and revocable by the will of the states, "who alone are truly sovereign" and "possess supreme dominion." Stating that "it would be difficult to sustain" this interpretation of the Constitution's origins, Marshall spent much of *McCulloch* arguing against it. While it was true that the framers may have been elected by state legislatures, he argued, the proposed Constitution that emerged from Philadelphia nonetheless required ratification. To become the nation's supreme law, it first had to gain the approval of the American people, who were perfectly able to accept or reject the Constitution, acting on their decision "in the only manner in which they can act safely, effectively and wisely, on such a subject—by assembling in convention" (403). All of America was assembled there, if only in symbol. State ratifying conventions hardly indicated the ultimate sovereignty of the individual states, but were instead a concession to the practical impossibility of "breaking down the lines which separate the States." Put simply, the mode of adoption did not detract from the Constitution's authority as proceeding "directly from the people." Indeed, as Marshall declared, the document was "ordained and established in the name of the people," and what came into existence was "emphatically and truly, a Government of the people" (405).

Marshall's theory of the Constitution's ratification went hand in glove with his argument on behalf of the authority of the national government. His argument began with a discussion of those aspects of the Constitution that indicated its national sovereignty. Because the people intended the Constitution to institute "effective government" and not a mere league between sovereign states, the powers of the national government were "to be exercised directly" on the people and for their common benefit (17 U.S. 405). In matters of textual interpretation, and particularly as applied to the question of the Bank's constitutionality, this intention called for giving the words of the Constitution a construction befitting a national document. While admitting that, among the enumerated powers of the Constitution, "we do not find that of establishing a bank or creating a corporation," and noting that neither the words "Bank" nor "incorporation" could be found anywhere in the Constitution, he nevertheless sharply disagreed with Maryland's argument that the Bank was thus illegitimate, arguing that, if adopted, the defendants' narrow construction of the Constitution would so weaken Congress that its enumerated powers "would be nugatory" (406, 413).[18] Instead, the intention of the American people "to form a more perfect union" and establish a national government conducive to their prosperity and happiness meant "ample means" must be given to the government to execute its constitutional powers and duties (404, 408). Thus the incorporation of the Bank, as well as the creation of state branches, represented a legitimate "choice of means" to execute the powers granted by the Constitution to effect the public good (419).

Having upheld the constitutionality of the Bank, Marshall then turned to the matter of Maryland's bank tax. It was here he dealt a direct blow to the hopes of Maryland and its doctrine of state sovereignty. While granting that the states exercised taxation powers concurrently with the national government, he claimed the Constitution could restrain even this "vital" authority in cases where its use was "in its nature incompatible with, and repugnant to, the constitutional laws of the Union" (17 U.S. 425). Counsel for the Bank had argued the Maryland tax was just such a case, and Marshall agreed, remarking that the Bank's "claim has been sustained on a principle which so entirely pervades the Constitution, is so intermixed with the materials which compose it, so interwoven with its web, so blended with its texture, as to be incapable of being separated from it without rending it into shreds" (426). This fundamental principle, he continued, "is that the Constitution and the laws made in pursuance thereof are supreme; that they control the Constitution and laws of the respective States, and cannot be controlled by them." Such a "great principle," which according to Marshall might "be almost termed an axiom," entailed three corollary rules: first, "that a power to create implies a power to preserve"; second, "that a power to destroy, if wielded by a different hand, is hostile to, and incompatible with these powers to create and to preserve"; and finally, "where this repugnancy exists, that authority which is supreme must control, not yield to that over which it is supreme." Connecting these dots to the case at hand led to a clear conclusion: the Maryland tax imposed on the operations of the Second Bank was unconstitutional.

Reinforcing Marshall's immediate judgment in *McCulloch* are his more philosophic reflections concerning the sovereignty of the national government. Here his nationalism seems to rise to new heights. On those occasions when national and state power came into conflict, Marshall claimed, it was crucial to the nation that the "authority which is supreme must control, not yield to that over which it is supreme" (17 U.S. 426). By his lights, the controlling authority of national law over conflicting state law was unambiguous. Thus he forcefully declared the Court's "conviction" that the states "have no power, by taxation or otherwise, to retard, impede, burthen, or in any manner control the operations of the constitutional laws enacted by Congress to carry into effect the powers vested in the national Government" (436). This proposition concerning the government's sovereignty was an irrefutable truth, however much it was denied by the states rights' supporters' attempt at political football. Indeed, Marshall emphasized, it was of "the very essence of supremacy" to remove any and all "obstacles to its action within its own sphere, and so to modify every power vested in subordinate governments" that would interfere with the exercise of its powers. This principle of supremacy, he added, must always be kept in view while "construing" the Constitution (427). In his heart did he sense that his words would also be construed by opponents in the not so distant future?

McCulloch on Federalism

Political sovereignty has not always been defined in absolute terms.[19] As early as 1774, notions of federal and confederal political arrangements were frequently being proposed by radical republicans in the American colonies.[20] According to Bernard Bailyn, because these thinkers located ultimate sovereign authority in the hands of the people, they were able to see the idea in more complex and multidimensional terms, so that with independence they were free to experiment with more centrifugal forms of political and legal power.[21] By 1787, federalism had become an accepted principle, clearly expressed by Madison in his *Federalist* #39, where he argued that states were "no more subject, within their respective spheres, to the general authority, than the general authority is subject to them, within its own sphere."[22] Yet in spite of such declarations, federalism in the early republic presented new dilemmas, as jurisdictional challenges involving state and national government unsettled even the most carefully constructed theories throughout the 1790s.[23] Hence constitutional thinkers were faced with the challenge of elaborating a coherent conception of federalism, a challenge that Marshall responded to in *McCulloch*. Indeed, Ira Strauber has gone so far as to call the opinion "the classic statement" of American federalism, "a weave of pragmatic and political theoretical arguments about underdetermined sovereignty interests that mute the force of arguments for state and shared sovereignty without, however, altogether undermining claims for state power."[24]

Two arguments were central to Marshall's defense of federalism in *McCulloch*: the limitations the Constitution imposed on national law and the coordinate legislative powers exercised by both national and state government.[25] He begins with the restrictions the Constitution placed on national policy making. Though *McCulloch* put forward a broad reading of congressional power in its legal justification of the Second Bank, it did not extend to Congress free rein to pass any law that might be tangentially related to its constitutional powers. Provisos and limitations on congressional authority abounded, the opinion stressed, and it was the duty of the Court to enforce those limits whenever they were breached. Even more remarkable is that Marshall's statement of this commitment occurs in his discussion of the implied powers of Congress. All must admit, he announced, that the powers of the national government were limited, and that such limits "are not to be transcended" (17 U.S. 421). In this regard, he cited a number of qualifications governing the constitutionality of any given statute. The first condition governed the object or end of legislation, which must be "legitimate" and "within the scope of the Constitution." Simply meeting this threshold, however, did not guarantee the constitutionality of legislation. A second provision went further, declaring that the sole means that may be employed by Congress to implement legitimate objects were those "which are appropriate, which are plainly adapted to that end, which are not prohibited, but consist with the letter and spirit of the Constitution." Marshall did not issue a blank check to Congress, but couched his endorsement of the legality of the Bank in terms designed to govern and delimit the constitutionality of national policy. Where his latter-day critics have seen language fraught with ambiguity, for Marshall the qualifications governing constitutional means and ends limited both what the national government might do and how it might do it.

Federalism was also protected by the very composition of the national government. Congress, Marshall suggested, was not the only political power states had to fear. As he pointed out, a large national legislature afforded to each individual state protection from the invasions of another state. It was a bit of a change in tone from his warnings about "legislative omnipotence" in *Marbury*. Noting the fact that "in the Legislature of the Union alone are all represented," he held that it was only reasonable that Congress rather than the states was entrusted with the power of governing those "measures which concern all" (17 U.S. 431). Jealous of its power, one state would hardly turn over to another state the authority to control even the most insignificant of its operations, let alone the power of taxation. To solve this impasse, the national government would be entrusted with those matters that concerned all citizens, and like state legislatures, its representatives would be held accountable by the citizens of the United States for abusing that trust. Thus, because "the people of all the States, and the States themselves, are represented in Congress," a state interfering with the operations of the national government acted not only on its own constituents but also attacked other states and those "people over whom they claim no control" (435). If threats to state sovereignty were what state governments feared most, Marshall suggested, they needed as much protection against other states as they did against the national government.

Proceeding to his second argument, Marshall allowed that the states were not only protected by the federal system, but they also possessed considerable power and autonomy of their own under its aegis. In particular, state governments retained a pivotal set of political powers to regulate their domestic affairs. The dispersal of such power could scarcely be avoided in a large country. And so, to the extent that state law did not conflict with the paramount law of the Constitution, all such laws were legitimate and due full obedience. The opinion went out of its way to emphasize that even the power of taxation was reserved to the states, notwithstanding the Court's particular annulment of the Maryland bank tax. As Marshall reminded his readers, "the power of taxation is one of vital importance" and "is retained by the States" (17 U.S. 425). Neither the Supreme Court nor the Constitution had altered the exercise of this power by the state governments: "that it is not abridged by the grant of a similar power to the Government of the Union; [and] that it is to be concurrently exercised by the two Governments" were not merely opinions, but "truths" that had "never been denied" by the Court.

Thus the Maryland statute was not invalidated because it trespassed on a power that belonged exclusively to the national government. For Marshall, the illegality of the state tax turned on its specific disruption of the operations of the Second Bank, "an instrument employed by the

Government of the Union to carry its powers into execution" (17 U.S. 436–37). As with *Marbury*, the conflict between two laws was key, and perhaps the Court's decision would have been quite different had the Maryland law not posed such a direct affront to national law. Indeed, sounding a note of reassurance to the states, Marshall emphasized that the *McCulloch* verdict had not altered the basic balance of power between the states and the national government as defined by the Constitution. The Court's ruling, he declared, "does not deprive the States of any resources which they originally possessed" (436). Apparently in a spirit of friendly support, Marshall even went so far as to list constitutionally valid forms of taxation that remained at Maryland's disposal: the real property of the bank as well as interest held by its customers were both fit objects of state taxation, "in common with other property of the same description throughout the state" (317). Here is how you might exact your revenge, Marshall intimated. Such remarks suffice to show that he did not simply dismiss either the role of the states or state legislatures as integral pieces of the constitutional order. For Marshall, political power was distributed and shared between state and national government, and in defending the Bank he was careful not to undermine the legitimacy of the many state banks or the valid measures state governments might otherwise enact to curb the Bank's influence. Seen in this light, the crux of *McCulloch* was not Marshall's nationalism, but his nuanced theory of federalism.

Beyond Nationalism and Federalism: Defining Constitutional Sovereignty

Nevertheless, Marshall's constitutionalism cannot be captured by the language of nationalism or federalism alone. For Marshall, neither the powers nor the policies of government stood as the nation's supreme legal authority. Instead, this authority belonged to the Constitution itself. The document was more than a guarantor of national supremacy or federalism, because it embodied more than the supremacy clause or the Tenth Amendment. In the tug of war between opponents and supporters of the Second Bank, Americans risked losing sight of the controlling authority of the entire Constitution over the political process. Its words, not the statutes of Congress or the state legislatures, were sovereign.[26] Ultimately, Marshall believed this was the essential principle on which his audience should refocus in the battle over the Bank.

Marshall's theory of constitutional sovereignty is implicit in *McCulloch* but is brought into greater light in the essays that he wrote in its wake. The first two of these pseudonymous essays, written by "A Friend to the Union," appeared in the *Philadelphia Union* and the *Alexandria Gazette*. Nine others, authored by "A Friend of the Constitution," soon followed in the *Gazette and Alexandria Daily Advertiser*.[27] In these articles, Marshall penned a spirited defense of *McCulloch* that was at once precise and comprehensive. Nor were the essays purely partisan sensations, as might be expected from their popular political setting. Rather, they reflect the depth of seriousness the Chief Justice showed toward public perceptions of the Supreme Court in particular and the Constitution in general. Apprehensive that the words of Virginia's states' rights proponents would prove fatal to the Constitution if left unanswered, Marshall meticulously justified the *McCulloch* decision and defended the reputation of the Supreme Court. But of even greater significance, these articles represent a robust argument on behalf of the Constitution's sovereignty.[28]

One does not need to look far to see what events motivated Marshall to write the essays. The bank kerfuffle was, in a manner of speaking, a family affair. When Marshall returned to his Richmond home in the summer of 1819, animosity toward the Supreme Court in the state of Virginia was running at a fever pitch. The Richmond Junto spirited the uproar. On March 30th, the Democratic-Republican *Richmond Enquirer* entered the fray. By way of introduction, Thomas Ritchie, the paper's editor-in-chief, announced to readers that a series of essays would appear in the coming weeks responding to the "alarming errors" of the Supreme Court.[29] The first two essays that appeared were most likely written by Virginia Judge William Brockenbrough, a stanch defender of Virginia sovereignty, employing the pen name "Amphictyon." Then, beginning on June 11, four more articles were published warning readers of the danger the Marshall Court posed to the states, this time authored by Judge Spencer Roane of the Virginia Court of Appeals (and son-in-law of Patrick Henry), who employed the pseudonym "Hampden."[30] By mid-summer, encouraged by a resolution passed by the Virginia legislature formally repudiating the *McCulloch* decision, public criticism of the case was escalating into open defiance of the Court's decision. Marshall followed this trend anxiously. As he confided to his fellow justice Joseph Story, "our opinion in the bank case has roused the sleeping spirit of Virginia—if indeed it ever sleeps." Correctly predicting the opinion would be "attacked in the papers with some asperity," he went on to lament that the Court's supporters "never write for the public." By leaving the field to those who would cast the opinion in the worst possible light, he feared, the opinion would soon "be considered as *damnably heretical*."[31] Concerned that the very existence of the still frag- ile Constitution was at stake, Marshall made a decision in response to a charged atmosphere that would not permit itself to be ignored: he would not let the battery of attacks pass in silence.[32]

Marshall began by acknowledging the difficulty of the case. Writ- ing as "A Friend of the Constitution," he warned that great constitutional questions must sometimes require "a course of intricate and abstruse rea- soning, which it requires no inconsiderable degree of mental exertion to comprehend" ("Friend," 156).[33] Thus the Court's opinions could be easily and grossly misrepresented, and the case of *McCulloch* in particular pre- sented "the fairest occasion for wounding mortally, the vital powers of the government, thro' its judiciary." To no small degree, the essays clarified, expanded on, and reinforced points raised by Marshall in *McCulloch* to parry the attacks delivered against the Court. Let us consider one example. In the opinion, Marshall had stated that the Court would render the final determination of the constitutionality of legislation, and he mentioned in passing that its affirmative judgment on the constitutionality of the Second Bank could very well change on future occasions. As he warned, should Congress "adopt measures which are prohibited by the Constitution" or "pass laws not intrusted to the Government," then "it would become the painful duty of this tribunal, should a case requiring such a decision come before it, to say that such an act was not the law of the land" (17 U.S. 423).[34] It seems this point required some underscoring. The express words of the Court in *McCulloch*, he now reiterated, limit the discretion of Congress to such means for executing laws "as are appropriate" in the Court's judgment ("Friend," 187). Thus Marshall was not simply breaking new ground in the essays, but returning to and retracing old arguments as well—especially those points in *McCulloch* that might allay fears about the centralizing tendencies of a powerful national government.

Taking full advantage of his anonymity, Marshall next set his sights on Brockenbrough and Roane. Declaring that "zealous and persevering hostility" toward the national government had lately been stirred up in Virginia, Marshall responded to Roane's "ranting declamation," with its "rash impeachment" of the integrity of the Court, contrasting it with his own clear-sighted "investigation of truth" ("Friend," 155, 157). He saw that his opponents were not interested in a serious discussion of principles, and both the tone and content of his writings reflect the acrimony of the occasion.

Yet even while responding to his critics' charges in point-by-point detail, a broader argument on behalf of the Constitution's sovereignty emerges. First, the Constitution was created by all Americans to accomplish objects that affected all citizens. Second, its supremacy was a matter of practical necessity: any state required an ultimate source of political authority. Finally, it secured rather than undermined the principles of limited government and federalism that were held dear by all citizens. These lines of argument form the core of Marshall's defense of *McCulloch* and, just as important, point to the broader political philosophy underlying the particulars of the case. Marshall saw his essays as a site for not simply answering the charges of his critics, but also developing a political theory concerning the Constitution's sovereignty.

To understand Marshall's constitutionalism in these articles, one must begin with his definition of the Constitution. Of course, Marshall had revealed some of this picture in *McCulloch*. There he had famously described the Constitution as a document intended by its framers "to endure for ages to come" that consequently must "be adapted to the various *crises* of human affairs" along with those national "exigencies" the framers themselves could only have dimly perceived (17 U.S. 415). By its nature, a constitution was a document containing principles that were left intentionally open-ended for purposes of their application, and thus "only its great outlines should be marked" and "its important objects designated" (407). While it did set forth focal points for organizing government, the document was ultimately a forward-looking charter, not a detailed contract. It did not stand for a mere tinkering with the status quo, but created a nation whose final contours its framers could not fully foresee. Setting forth in strict and precise terms the actions that the national government could and could not perform, listing in "accurate detail" the several "subdivisions of which its great powers will admit, and of all the means by which they may be carried into execution," would have given the Constitution "the prolixity of a legal code." Such a document would be scarcely comprehensible to the human mind, and "would probably never be understood by the public." Generality was therefore a basal element of written constitutions, and it was the obligation of the Court to exercise its judgment concerning the legality of the "minor ingredients" deduced from the nature of the Constitution's grand objects (407).

Writing as "Friend," however, Marshall went further than simply to claim the Court must be flexible in its interpretation of the constitutional powers of the national government. First and foremost, the Constitution was created through a partnership between fellow citizens, not a peace agreement among sworn opponents. Such "a contract between enemies seeking each other's destruction" would make its parties "anxious to insert every particular, lest a watchful adversary should take advantage of the omission" ("Friend," 170). Moreover, the Constitution was not akin to a zero-sum agreement between private individuals "wherein implications in favor of one man impair[ed] the vested rights of another." Hence, it differed from "the cases put in the books of the common law," which were unconcerned with constitutional government (169). In positive terms, the Constitution "is the act of a people, creating a government without which they cannot exist as a people" (170). An excessively cramped reading of Congressional power would debilitate the charter's purpose as "a general system for all future times, to be adapted by those who administer it." Give up the "unnatural or restricted construction of the constitution" pressed by the Court's foes, Marshall implored (198)! Reiterating that "from its nature, such an instrument can describe only the great objects it is intended to accomplish, and state in general terms the specific powers which are deemed necessary for those objects," Marshall described members of Congress as ultimately beholden to its rule, not to their own. To fulfill the "great objects" proclaimed in the Constitution, the office of a legislature is created, and as an emanation of the people, it was responsible for navigating, "according to the judgment of the nation," its course "within those great outlines which are given in the constitution" (170, 171). The Second Bank, whose legitimacy was so forcefully justified on the specific basis of Congress' implied powers in *McCulloch*, is defended to a greater degree in the essays based on the ultimate authority of the Constitution.

Marshall also viewed the Constitution as playing a creative role in solidifying American national identity, a point he would dwell on in greater detail in the Native American cases years later. Having denied that the union was simply a product of individual states, he now claimed that it was the Constitution that had given Americans a new "theoretical or constitutional existence"—one comparable to the national identity of the French, no less ("Friend," 195). On those occasions dealing with "national affairs," such as matters of war and peace, this identity was most evident. But the language of the Constitution also suggested that its existence was both more pervasive and more commonplace. Hence, Marshall pointed out, a Senator must have been a "citizen of the United States" for seven years, and the oath taken by every adopted citizen was to the United States. Such provisions proved, in his words, that "we are all citizens, not only of our particular states, but also of this great republic." The Constitution was much more than a document that specified the exercise of legitimate political authority, and as we have seen in the *Marbury* opinion, its function went beyond its status as a practical rulebook for the nation. Something more creative was at work in its rule. Pay no mind to those who would attempt "to render the terms *American people* and *national government* odious," he admonished (198). As a written testament to the national identity of the American people, the Constitution played a formative role in constructing an enduring constitutional citizenship that could not be confined to the vocabulary of either national or state membership. Its words confirmed that "the people of these states are also the people of the United States" (195). But, Marshall avowed, these two characters, far from being at odds with each other, are joined together and even "identified" in "the language of the Constitution."

Marshall carefully but forcefully argued that so long as the Constitution governed the nation's affairs, a despotic national power was a mere scarecrow conjured up by *McCulloch*'s critics. Dispelling their fear tactics entailed reframing the basic terms of debate employed by Marshall's foes, for the national government and the idea of supremacy itself were gaining poor reputations in Virginia. Through lexical sleight of hand, Marshall argued, Roane had consistently "confounded *supremacy* with *despotism*," but in fact supremacy simply meant "highest in authority," an authority that may or may not abuse its legitimate powers ("Friend," 187). Turning to the constitutional text, he asked: "Is not the government of the union, 'within its sphere of action,' 'supreme,' or 'highest in authority'? This is certainly the fact, and is certainly the language of the Constitution." After all, Marshall continued, in national affairs, "what authority is above it?" (188). But, far from being unchecked, the policies of the national government were tethered to those restraints imposed by the Constitution, a document that could also be lessened, expanded, or otherwise amended under extraordinary circumstances. As he reminded his readers, "The constitution may be changed, any constitution may be changed." In the United States, one need look no further than the amendment process spelled out in Article V. Supreme power could be altered and reformed, unlike despotic power, which operated without the hindrance of popular checks or institutional balances, and for whom constitutions were mere parchment. Marshall's response to Roane's portrayal of an all-powerful national government was at once direct and reassuring: so long as it remained the nation's supreme law, the Constitution was a strong barrier against a return of tyranny to America.

The Constitution's protection of the principle of federalism is the final pillar of Marshall's newspaper defense of *McCulloch*. A common refrain in both Maryland's as well as Brockenbrough's argument against the Bank was the notion that the states, not the American people, had authorized the Constitution. Brockenbrough had gone to great lengths to prove that the several states "not only gave birth to the constitution, but its life depended on the existence of the state governments" ("Amphictyon," 56). For evidence, he called to mind the historical record of the Constitution's creation: the federal convention was populated by delegates appointed by the state legislatures, the document was submitted for ratification to state conventions, and these conventions represented the states acting "in their highest political, and sovereign authority." For Brockenbrough, there could be no mistake: the Constitution "was adopted and brought into existence" by the states, who had surrendered none of their original sovereignty upon its ratification. Citing the example of Rhode Island's initial reluctance to ratify, he noted that the Constitution was not binding on any state, even the smallest in population, until that state had given its free consent. In the course of distorting the history of the Constitution's ratification, he continued, the Court had moved to substitute the American people for the states as the source of the Constitution's authority. This seemingly uncontroversial principle entailed grave consequences, including dismissing the role of the state governments and leaving a minority of Americans at the mercy of majority rule—or majority tyranny—as exercised by all citizens in Congress (55). Here was a core argument of *Federalist #10*, now turned back upon its Federalist proponents. It was the states and not the measures of the national government that might be overrun by factions bent on insidious interests.

For Marshall, however, Brockenbrough was tilting at windmills. Nobody had denied that the states continued to play an important policy role under the Constitution, just as they had under the Articles of Confederation. But Brockenbrough's more serious error once again involved his way with words, in this instance his conflation of the term "national" with "consolidation" ("Friend," 193).[35] The principle that the United States was a federal and not a consolidated government was "universally known and universally admitted. No person in his senses ever has, ever will, or ever can controvert it" (191). Brockenbrough had hastily assumed that state sovereignty had been invalidated along with the bank tax, accusing Marshall of throwing the baby out with the bathwater. The states were key to the Constitution's creation, Marshall emphasized, but they did not determine its fundamental character. For Marshall, the nature and language of a legal document, not simply its mode of adoption, were the hallmarks that determined its identity. Put differently, in assessing the authority of federal law, more factors must be weighed than just the manner in which the Constitution was made. The powers of the national government depended not on the Constitution "being adopted by the people acting in a single body, or in single bodies." Rather, "the character of a government depends on its constitution" in a more general sense (197).

What exactly was Marshall getting at? As he saw it, the language of the document itself must be examined to ascertain the type of political and legal order it envisioned for the nation. As he put it, "the words of an instrument, unless there be some sinister design which shuns the light, will always represent the intention of those who frame it" ("Friend," 199). And the words of the Constitution's preamble could not be clearer in declaring that the Constitution was the creation of the American people, and not the several states. In his words, "an instrument intended to be the act of the people, will purport to be the act of the people," while, conversely, "an instrument intended to be the act of the states, will purport to be the act of the states." Thus the Constitution clearly cast the people as those who create and define the government, while the Articles of Confederation "was intended to be the act of the states, and was drawn in language comporting with that intention" (85). The difference between the respective origins of these documents could hardly have been starker. It was entirely evident, he concluded, that "our constitution is not a league. It is a government; and has all the constituent powers of a government" (199).

Like his opponents, Marshall was not above leaning on the power of rhetoric to warn his readers of the consequences of rejecting the Constitution's sovereignty. Disregarding its supreme authority would have untold repercussions, not the least of which would be throwing the country into a state of anarchy even more perilous than conditions under the weak Articles of Confederation. It is not inconceivable, Marshall mused, "that the constitution may be so expounded by its enemies as to become totally inoperative" and a dead letter ("Friend," 160). Perhaps the only way to appease critics of *McCulloch*, Marshall speculated, would be to allow the individual states to become policy gatekeepers, passing judgment on each law proposed by the national government and consequently clogging the business of state and national government alike.[36] Thus "a new mode of amendment, by way of report of committees of a state legislature and resolutions thereon, may pluck from" the Constitution "power after power" in piecemeal fashion. Yet an even graver scenario might be imagined. State legislatures may choose to completely "sweep off the whole" Constitution and the powers it bestowed, appointing instead whatever "scanty and inconvenient means" they thought fit for the national government to fulfill its great responsibilities. Whether the powers of the national government were reduced gradually or all at once, however, the result of leaving to the states the power of constitutional authority and interpretation would be the same. States' rights theory, Marshall admonished, would eviscerate both the national government and the Constitution, leaving the document "an inanimate corpse, incapable of effecting any of its objects." Such was the logical consequence of states' rights arguments. A far safer course would be to entrust judgments of constitutionality to the Supreme Court, Marshall claimed, for there was no body or tribunal less liable to be "swayed by unworthy motives" from the performance of its sworn duties (212). Behind the veil of anonymity, the Chief Justice minced no words: the Court, not the states, was the best defense against either legislative tyranny or a return to an impotent confederation.

With regard to *McCulloch*, Marshall's *Gazette* essays underscore familiar themes while drawing attention to new ones in his political thought. For Marshall, the Constitution represented much more than a new legal order for a new nation. It symbolized the civic responsibility and integrity of the American people, standing as a reminder to new generations of the patriotism that led to its creation. In making this argument, Marshall would drop his characteristic detachment as Chief Justice, driving his argument home in vivid and passionate terms. Seeing the "weakness" of the Articles of Confederation, he claimed, the American people had chosen to "cement" their fragile union by means of a new national charter. Their decision to change the Articles "into an effective government" was a testament to the "wisdom and patriotism of our country," freeing the American people from political difficulties that would only reappear if the proponents of states' rights doctrine had their way ("Friend," 200). As Marshall summarizes in his concluding essay, more than the scope of congressional authority was at stake in *McCulloch*. The attacks on the Court were "intended to produce a very serious effect," one that in his judgment could lead to the Constitution's "utter subversion," in which its sovereignty was prostrated "at the feet of its members" (214). Roane's states' rights diatribes threatened the powers of national government and indeed the principles of federalism. But beyond even these targets, still more was at stake in the rhetorical battle over *McCulloch*. As Marshall described, the Constitution itself was imperiled by the states' rights rhetoric. To overturn the concept of constitutional sovereignty, he believed, was to put at risk this nascent nation the framers—moreover, the people themselves—had worked so diligently to construct. Deny the concept and you deny the Constitution, Marshall believed, and the nation would be left with no ultimate law at all. Whether writing as Chief Justice or "A Friend of the Constitution," Marshall was determined not to let that happen without a fight.

Conclusions

Unlike *Marbury*, Marshall's political philosophy in *McCulloch* and its aftermath dealt foremost with constitutional sovereignty, not legitimacy, although the two concepts are not to be viewed discretely.[37] Indeed, themes that were elemental to Marshall's thinking in *Marbury*—particularly ideas of popular sovereignty and the Constitution's settlement function—continued to loom large in *McCulloch*'s discussion of federalism. But *McCulloch* and Marshall's showdown with the Richmond Junto does not simply reiterate Marshall's earlier argument. Occurring sixteen years following his opinion in *Marbury*, the row over the Second Bank represents Marshall's entry into a timely and also timeless debate over political sovereignty. Rather than fidelity to the Constitution, the question now turned on how the Constitution sanctioned or proscribed acts of the federal and state policy. Moreover, Marshall's manner in these two episodes is quite different. In *Marbury*, Marshall hammers home his argument regarding legitimacy; in *McCulloch*, he applies a scalpel to his antagonists' arguments to quell fears being raised regarding consolidation and despotism.

Notwithstanding this more methodical approach, Marshall's opinion in *McCulloch* will continue to be a source of controversy. Many nationalist interpretations of the opinion will continue to diminish Marshall's defense of state authority and limitations on national policy, while arguments that emphasize *McCulloch*'s federalism will continue to understate Marshall's concern for a robust national government with the capability to execute its laws. But these interpretations must acknowledge that the linchpin of Marshall's political thought was neither nationalism nor federalism, but constitutionalism. In pitting the state legislatures against the national government and local policy against national legislation, Marshall's critics had too often neglected the Constitution's sovereign authority over both spheres of authority. After all, in *McCulloch* it was this document, not the national government, whose principles must "be adapted to the various *crises* of human affairs" (17 U.S. 415). It was the Constitution, not the states or general government, that was the nation's ultimate legal authority. And it was the Constitution, not the political branches—not even the Supreme Court—that was an engine for government, not "a splendid bauble" (421).

But only by turning to Marshall's *Gazette* essays do we see the full picture of his commitment to the Constitution. For the essays reveal a figure concerned with solidifying its sovereignty in the court of law and the court of public opinion alike. Beyond the facts in *McCulloch*, beyond even the principles of national authority and federalism so ably expounded in the Court's opinion, it is the essays that convey Marshall's reconfiguration of sovereignty under the Constitution. Only under its rule, with its sovereignty neither wholly unified in national power nor wholly divided among the states, could rival political authorities and theories of sovereignty coexist peacefully. At the same time, so long as the Constitution remained supreme law, each of the nation's political branches would have little reason for apprehension concerning the exercise of political power. The document's careful definition and division of "the powers of the government" created an institutional and legal "equipoise," one "which its framers, and the American people, believed to be most conducive to the public happiness and to public liberty" ("Friend," 160).

Throughout the essays, Marshall was careful to elevate the Constitution above ordinary legislation passed by Congress or the states. Recall that the document existed as a great national charter, not a detailed policy statement. It did not simply promulgate rules for an existing nation, but created a new one. And far from setting itself up as a rival to either national or state governments, it demarcated and secured their particular domains of authority. While Marshall's regard for the Constitution is in itself unsurprising, in the *Gazette* essays he gives flesh to his belief in its ultimate sovereignty, explaining in a public forum the lineaments of this dimension of his political theory. It was this principle of constitutional sovereignty, which cannot be collapsed into nationalism or federalism alone, that he clung to in *McCulloch* and throughout his time on the Court.[38] This aspect of his political theory, as well as the essays in which it was developed, merit greater recognition than they have hitherto received.

As Americans continue to debate matters involving federalism, it is good sense to keep in mind Marshall's commitment to the Constitution's sovereignty. So long as the laws of Congress trigger backlash, the question of where state authority ends and national authority begins is one that will continue to provoke considerable argument. It is only right that we consider *McCulloch*'s relevance to this ongoing dialogue. In doing so we should draw upon not only the majority opinion itself, but the arguments that occurred outside the courtroom as well, for these too shaped our constitutional development. Marshall's essays in the popular press show that he believed the Constitution's sovereignty could provide common ground for proponents of a strong national government as well as principled federalists. Thus interpretations of *McCulloch* that rely exclusively on either nationalism or federalism go too far in simplifying the Chief Justice's thought. After all, he never pledged his utmost loyalty to the national government. Nor was federalism the chief object of his devotion. We must never forget that above all else the object he was expounding—and defending—was the Constitution. In both the *McCulloch* decision and its public defense, Marshall had delivered states' rights theory a punch—but, as we will see in the next chapter, it was not a fatal blow.

3

———————

John Marshall, *Ogden v. Saunders*, and the Character of Constitutional Liberty

No Supreme Court justice has left a deeper impression on the legal foundations of the American economy than John Marshall. Many of his most memorable opinions bear on matters related to economic development. In *Fletcher v. Peck* (1810), he defended the sanctity of the contract clause against attempts by the state of Georgia to repeal the sale of millions of acres of land in the Yazoo River territory. In *Dartmouth College v. Woodward* (1819), he supported Dartmouth College against political efforts to revoke the institution's private charter, in doing so laying the groundwork for the expansion of private corporate enterprise free from the meddling of state legislatures. And in *Gibbons v. Ogden* (1824), he struck down a New York steamboat monopoly, winning national acclaim and affirming the constitutional authority of Congress to regulate commerce among the states. Francis Stites minced no words when describing the Chief Justice's economic philosophy. While the states possessed "some power over economic development," Marshall believed that when individual state and national economic interests conflicted, "the Supreme Court would make the final choice" concerning which interest prevailed. From where Marshall sat, that choice was clear: "National supremacy and economic policy went hand in hand."[1]

As a result of Marshall's influence in such cases, it is all too common to overlook those rare occasions when his legal views on commerce failed to carry the day. *Ogden v. Saunders* (1827) was arguably the most important of those instances, marking Marshall's lone dissent on a constitutional question in his thirty-four years on the nation's high court. The background of the case involved the technical details of contract law and insolvency, but for Marshall, much larger stakes were involved. The case, he believed, went to the philosophical heart of the nation's liberal and republican foundations. But of even greater significance, he believed that the survival of constitutional liberty itself was jeopardized by the Court's decision. In *Ogden*, Marshall registered more than mild disagreement concerning the extent of contractual obligation. He examined the power of contract and the duty of performance, and he anchored these concepts to the constitutional republicanism he believed essential for securing the nation's burgeoning economy.

This constitutional republicanism differed from classical understandings of republicanism grounded in heroic sacrifice or steadfast commitment to the common good. Marshall's republicanism was of a different cast, calling forth an understanding of the Constitution as providing a shield against the ever present threat of political domination. Unlike many contemporary theories of political domination, however, Marshall was especially sensitive to the dangers the passions of the moment posed to economic liberty and its promotion of norms of trust and responsibility. In truth, Marshall's political thought in his dissent is neither wholly liberal nor republican, but committed to a way of seeing citizenship and economic exchange that resisted traditional categorization.

Students of Marshall's thought have long stressed his devotion to classical liberal principles, notably the protection of property rights and a free-market economy. Vernon Parrington noted that the "two fixed conceptions which dominated Marshall during his long career on the bench were the sovereignty of the federal state and the sanctity of private property."[2] Similarly, Max Lerner claimed that Marshall sought "to fight the battles of the propertied group," securing private property rights "from governmental encroachment."[3] The decision of *Ogden v. Saunders* in particular has been seen as a hallmark of his classical liberalism. Robert Faulkner sees his *Ogden* dissent as "beset with difficulties" but allows that, when "pruned of its problems," its conclusion is that the free market must be limited only "according to the needs of commerce itself and of a commercial society." Marshall was convinced, Faulkner declares, that "the public interest is served by fundamental *laissez faire*, by essentially free exchange."[4] Joseph Konefsky makes a similar point in his discussion of *Ogden*, asserting that it was Marshall's conviction "that it was the duty of the Supreme Court to protect America's economic community."[5] Taking a broader view of Marshall's jurisprudence, Richard Matthews reaches similar conclusions: while accepting that there are several "not necessarily incompatible" interpretations of Marshall's constitutional thought, he argues that "in the end, his liberalism wins out" and concludes that, like "Hobbes, Locke, Hamilton, and Madison, Marshall is a nondemocratic liberal."[6]

We should hesitate before grouping Marshall among such diverse company. Indeed, in contrast to those who emphasize Marshall's commitment to personal rights, many scholars stress his concern with civic duty. According to Walter Berns, Marshall was "the greatest of the Supreme Court's republican schoolmasters," whose identification of the Constitution with the great figures of the founding period encouraged citizens to model their selflessness and patriotism on a smaller stage.[7] More recently, Kent Newmyer finds a "republican dimension" even in *Ogden v. Saunders*. "Call it morality, duty, or honor, Marshall believed those individuals who shared the benefits of the contract culture were also fully responsible for the contracts they made. And it was the duty of the law to make them so."[8] This emphasis on duty is echoed by another leading Marshall scholar, Thomas Shevroy, who argues that Marshall's republicanism saw the political world in Manichaean terms, divided "between the elements of virtue, goodness, and stable political order on the one hand, and those of vice, avarice, and passion on the other." The only viable force to counteract the latter phenomena was the willingness of the American people to dutifully follow the Constitution, a legal framework the Chief Justice believed set up "dikes" preventing political passions "from overwhelming stable order, at least for a time."[9] As G. Edward White put it, one of the main projects of the Court during the early nineteenth century was "that of preserving, perfecting, and modifying the exceptional American version of republicanism" evinced during the American Revolution.[10] For these authors, Marshall's republicanism emphasized citizens' obligations to the rule of law and one another, and one of his foremost objectives was to preserve a sense of duty to the United States and the Constitution in a time when threats to individual liberty assumed more subtle forms than the gun barrel.

Not content to rely exclusively on liberal or republican frameworks, some scholars have refused to classify Marshall within either of these traditions, insisting that his views were bound neither to rights-based liberalism nor to republican values. According to these authors, liberal conceptions of rights and republican notions of responsibility possessed little conceptual coherence during the politically tumultuous years of the

Marshall Court. Arguing against those who would cast Marshall as a modern liberal, Bruce Ackerman suggests that those interpretations that would cast Marshall as such miss their mark, noting "it would be laughable to assert that Alexander Hamilton and John Marshall did all the really tough work in elaborating the constitution of the modern welfare state."[11] James Ely Jr. also downplays Marshall's liberal credentials, contending that Marshall's emphasis on property rights was hardly atypical, but simply expressed "principles generally recognized as legitimate" by most Americans. On his view, the Court's decisions were part and parcel of "a broad consensus supportive of private property and contractual arrangements." Far from representing a courageous stance in defense of property rights, Ely suggests, Marshall's constitutional opinions appealed to "widely accepted norms" on those occasions when lawmakers "deviated from these principles."[12] In a similar vein, Stephen Siegel questions whether Marshall and his colleagues on the Court could have had any clear and unified theory of private property, given that the concept was characterized by confusion during Marshall's time.[13] Thanks to these more complex evaluations of Marshall's economic thinking, we can see why invocations of his legacy in more recent cases involving the contract clause appear at times muddled and even contradictory.[14]

However important the classifications of liberal or republican may be for understanding Marshall, few scholars have applied these terms to his dissent in *Ogden* in an extensive fashion.[15] This neglect results in an insufficient understanding of the philosophy that underpins Marshall's broader views on contract rights and state bankruptcy legislation. But, more important, we are left with an incomplete understanding of how Marshall transcended familiar categories of both classical liberalism and classical republicanism to defend a distinctive neo-republicanism based on the protection of individual liberties. To understand Marshall as a political thinker, one must firmly grasp his assimilation of elements of the liberal and republican traditions as it appears throughout his opinions. But one must also recognize his profound break from these traditions in his formulation of an understanding of freedom characterized by nondomination, a break especially apparent in the *Ogden* dissent. Marshall's view of the Constitution as safeguarding this new species of republican liberty was key to the argument he prosecuted against the Court's majority in *Ogden*. It was also a conception of liberty he believed was vital during the period of rapid economic growth of the 1820s.

Revisiting *Ogden v. Saunders*

Lewis Saunders, a merchant in Lexington, Kentucky, came to court demanding payment of a $2,200 debt arising from a contract signed by George Ogden, a citizen of Louisiana who lived in New York when the contract was signed. Ogden refused to pay, claiming he was discharged from the obligation by a New York bankruptcy law enacted in 1801. The statute allowed for prospective debtor relief, meaning that all legal contracts reached after the enactment would be subject to explicit regulations governing default. Once an insolvent debtor surrendered his or her assets, the individual was absolved from all future contractual obligations and was free to reenter the marketplace. Creditors had no recourse; in effect, they were stuck with the bill. To some, the state law provided the legislature with the ability to act quickly in the economic sphere in cases of emergency, allowing economic actors relief from undue financial hardship. To others, it was class legislation, benefiting debtors at the expense of creditors—a clear infringement of Article One's contract clause insofar as it altered the substance of future contracts. The main issue confronting the Court was not only whether Congress possessed the sole authority to enact bankruptcy laws, but also whether the New York statute was indeed in violation of the contract clause. Daniel Webster and longtime Supreme Court reporter Henry Wheaton, representing Saunders, argued forcefully that the clause prohibited bankruptcy laws that altered the performance of prospective as well as existing contracts. While broken contracts were subject to state regulation, that authority did not hold for those agreements not yet in default. Moreover, Webster claimed, the state law infringed upon the exclusive power of Congress to establish uniform laws governing bankruptcy throughout the United States. After all, he urged, a fundamental aim of the framers was to prevent state meddling in private economic affairs. Ogden's team of attorneys, led by Henry Clay, maintained that bankruptcy legislation was a concurrent power exercised by the states as well as the federal government under the Constitution. They had good authority for the claim. The team pointed to Marshall's dicta in the Court's earlier precedent set in *Sturges v. Crowinshield* (1819), where the Court acknowledged the principle of concurrent powers concerning bankruptcy in the course of invalidating another New York statute that retroactively altered the terms of contracts.[16]

On March 13, 1827, the Court upheld the New York legislation as constitutional. Justices Bushrod Washington, William Johnson, Smith

Thompson, and Robert Trimble each delivered lengthy opinions arguing that the fact that the law enacted provisions governing prospective default did not amount to a violation of the contract clause. Because provisions of the law preceded the creation of future contracts, so Marshall's longtime ally Washington argued, there was no actual impairment of existing contracts. Once passed, the New York law now became an integral part of all future contracts, implicitly known to and accepted by all parties. The hope was that such legislation might supply a general stabilizing influence on the nation's economy by casting a safety net to those entrepreneurs who were victims of bad luck (or, alternatively, those who had simply been foolhardy). For his part, Justice William Johnson, in his concurrent opinion, warned against focusing too much on economic rights at the expense of the national welfare, declaring that "the rights of all must be held and enjoyed in subserviency to the good of the whole," and the common good "must not be swallowed up and lost sight of while yielding attention to the claim of the creditor."[17]

Always solicitous that the Court project a united front, on this occasion Marshall could not go along with his fellow justices' reasoning. More surprisingly, however, was the fact that he could not let his disagreement pass in silence. In his first and last dissent on a constitutional question as Chief Justice, Marshall framed his argument based on what he saw as "the single question for consideration," namely, "whether the act of the State of New York is consistent with or repugnant to the constitution of the United States?" (25 U.S. 332).[18] Marshall disagreed sharply with his peers on the answer to this question, arguing that the statute not only violated the Constitution but also was unsound economic policy. Yet he was also hunting bigger game. In upholding the New York statute, the Court's majority had sided with economic expediency rather than the contract clause, the whims of public opinion rather than the stable rule of law. At the heart of Marshall's dissent lay deeper concerns about the ramifications of *Ogden*: concerns related to the security of rights, the importance of economic responsibility among citizens, and the legacy left by the framers of the Constitution. Appreciating these concerns propels us past the concepts of legitimacy and sovereignty into a direct encounter with the political theories regnant in Marshall's time and their relation to the type of republicanism he crafted in *Ogden*.

Marshall as Classical Liberal

For many scholars, classical liberal theory was the ideological lodestar for the American Revolution as well as the Constitution's creation. With its emphasis on protections of private property, personal freedom, and limited government, the language of John Locke was not simply one influence among many at the time of the founding: it provided the air that breathed life into the Constitution itself. Among the most famous of these treatments was the one offered by Louis Hartz, who argued that owing to its unique social conditions, North America staged a "nationalist articulation of Locke," a doctrine held with such unshakeable faith that alternatives to the nation's liberal tradition never took hold.[19] Indeed, as described by the historian John Diggins, so influential were classical liberal ideas on the American way of life that they constituted nothing less than the very "soul" of early American politics.[20] Indeed, for many eighteenth-century Americans, liberalism was not simply a theory but an absolute and often unreflective dogma, with its vocabulary of rights, property, and economic productivity forming the ethos of American political and social life. With the priority the doctrine gave to rights over duty, America appeared to enact a clean break with the classical republicanism of the past. As Michael Zuckert puts it, Americans were engaged in "not the discovery of, but the first attempt at, large-scale implementation of a rights-based politics."[21]

Judging by his dissent in *Ogden*, it seems that Marshall was an able spokesman for America's liberal tradition.[22] Certainly on the subject of how contracts were created, Marshall struck a distinctly Lockean chord. He was a strong defender of contract rights and private property throughout his life, a defense that took a dim view of excessive political intervention in the economy. Taking a position familiar to readers of Locke's *Second Treatise of Government*, he used his dissent in *Ogden* to look back to the past, tracing "the right to contract and the obligations created by contract" and finding their existence "anterior to and independent of society" (25 U.S. 345). These "original and preexisting principles" of contract dated to "the rudest state of nature," where "a man governs himself, and labors for his own purposes." In such primitive circumstances, what individuals acquired through physical labor became their own and could be either retained or transferred to another of their choosing. According to Marshall's description of the state of nature, these crude contractual agreements preceded society, because individuals in a state of nature possessed the right to form such agreements and enforce their terms independent of any conventional authority. "We find no allusion," he argued in *Ogden*, "from the earliest time, to any supposed act of the governing power giving obligation to contracts" (345). For Marshall, as for Locke, property, acquisition, trade, and commerce were all concepts and activities that government served rather than directed. Put simply, "contract and the obligations created by contract" were, "like many other natural rights, brought with man into society" (344, 345).[23]

When people moved from natural to civil society, government assumed the right to punish infringements of contracts, but played a minimal role in securing and enforcing private economic agreements. Restrictions placed on natural liberty and the responsibilities on the part of the government went hand in hand. While "force may rightfully be employed to coerce the party who has broken his engagement" in a state of nature, Marshall explained, when individuals "unite together and form a government," the individual surrenders his or her "right to enforce the observance of contracts" (25 U.S. 346). Political authority was a prerequisite for securing a "general peace"—plain and simple (350). Limited to enforcing contracts, government was never empowered to alter the terms reached by private individuals. As Marshall put it, the "degree of free agency" reserved to every individual even in civil society included "the right to contract," a right "not surrendered with the right to coerce performance" but appropriately "retained in its original extent" where left unregulated (350).

Yet Marshall's liberalism extended beyond the mere drawing of boundaries between civil authority and individual liberty. After all, the backdrop for his argument was not a crude state of nature, but the United States. Survey "the nature of our Union," Marshall urged, in all its geographic and economic diversity (25 U.S. 334). Regions that specialized in some commodities nonetheless stood in need of other goods. One could hardly fail to see that this heterogeneity was "intended to make us, in a great measure, one people, as to commercial objects."[24] Commercial exchange achieved this end, promoting the "intercommunication of individuals" and sundering "the lines of separation between states." Anticipating this eventuality, the framers of the Constitution concurred that "on the delicate subject of contracts once formed," the intervention of political officials "should be greatly abridged or entirely forbidden." For Marshall, commerce created bonds between individuals that transcended local, state, and even national memberships.

In *Ogden*, economic freedom, a narrow role for political authority over matters touching on private agreements, and the vitalization of a commercial society were the core elements of Marshall's classical liberalism. To no small extent, a judgment on the philosophy of John Locke is a judgment on Marshall's logic in *Ogden*. But for Marshall, even rights in the state of nature were not exercised absent concomitant duties and responsibilities. Notwithstanding the merits of liberalism, it downplayed the importance of a sense of obligation and trust in society's relationships. For Marshall, a strong sense of these responsibilities was essential for both the economic and civic stability of the nation, whether they linked political officials to voters or citizen to fellow citizen. Turning to these duties in his dissent entails turning to Marshall's sympathies with the classical republican tradition.

Marshall as Republican

In contrast to those who identify the United States with Lockean liberalism, many scholars look to early America and see a distinctly classical republican influence. A host of scholars has long highlighted the vocabulary of political power, corruption, and civic virtue prevalent throughout the founding era, tracing the genealogy of this language back to Anglo-Atlantic and Florentine republican traditions. Beginning in the 1950s, Clinton Rossiter, Neal Riemer, Douglas Adair, and Caroline Robbins were among the first to discuss the growth of radical republican ideology in England and its gradual transference to America.[25] Over the next decade, scholars such as Perry Miller, Cecelia Kenyon, and Richard Buel continued to clarify the salience of republican ideas in America.[26] But while these authors succeeded in challenging long-standing Lockean and Marxist interpretations of the founding era, they failed to clearly specify the changes in republicanism that occurred during the tradition's migration to North America. Bernard Bailyn was among the first to focus on republican strands of thought in the late colonial period, arguing that Americans eagerly embraced Whig notions of the duty of resistance to unchecked power.[27] Gordon Wood found even more of the vocabulary of corruption and resistance in late eighteenth-century America, while also stressing the equally important understandings of civic virtue, frugality, and the social solidarity on which republican government relied.[28] Building on the work of Bailyn and Wood, J. G. A. Pocock pushed back against the notion that the American founding was informed exclusively by the logic of Lockean liberalism or economic factors, suggesting that Americans were participants in an Atlantic republican tradition that stretched back to Machiavelli, Polybius, and even Aristotle.[29] To be sure, many scholars have argued that republican ideas in America were much less unified than the portrayals provided by Pocock and his fellow travelers would suggest.[30] Yet even in the absence of a settled meaning, well after the Constitution's ratification, as Lance Banning and others have argued, classical republican ideas retained a prominent place in the lexicon of many American thinkers.[31]

Much as Marshall was concerned with themes of liberal theory, his *Ogden* dissent also highlights key republican ideas. His classical republican sympathies emphasized the duty citizens owed each other, and those economic obligations that applied equally to all persons, regardless of background, wealth, or social standing. Once an agreement was entered, the fulfillment of its terms was irrevocable by political power, lest the fragile bonds uniting citizens be broken. This responsibility, generated "by the act of the parties" rather than positive law, harkened back to those basic treatises on the law of obligation and contract that had been the basis of America's legal system (25 U.S. 326).[32] In these works, Marshall claimed, one found general agreement "that contracts possess an intrinsic obligation, derived from the acts of free agents, and not given by government" (25 U.S. 350). The tie created by economic agreements—"the duty of keeping faith between . . . parties and the right to enforce it if violated"—entailed an obligation toward others that was carried by individuals into society, one that political officers should not disregard (345). Legislative attempts to modify this pre-political duty risked not only disrupting the very economic stability they sought to create, but also eroded the basis of a fundamental commitment incumbent upon all citizens.

Notwithstanding Marshall's emphasis on the minimal role of government in matters of contract, he also believed that legislators possessed real duties on behalf of the general public, even ones affecting the nation's economy. After all, a commercial society could not run on its own, but depended on statesmen committed to enacting laws that would maintain its success. Affording legal remedies when contractual obligations went unfulfilled was one such responsibility. Instituting statutes governing cases "of frauds, of usury, and of limitations" was among those other duties (25 U.S. 344). These minor exercises of "the external action of law upon contracts" constituted "the usual exercise of legislative power," one that refrained from "introducing conditions into them not agreed to by the parties" (343). It was the solemn duty of elected officials to address such aberrations in commercial exchange, and the "high sense of duty which men selected for the government of their fellow citizens must be supposed to feel" should furnish a guard "against a course of legislation which must end in self-destruction" for the country (352–53). The "solemn oath taken by every member to support the constitution of the United States," he warned, prohibited "intentional attempts to violate its spirit while evading its letter" (353). Thus, the failure to uphold the Constitution and afford a remedy to injured parties would be calamitous from an economic stand-point. Worse, dereliction of this "high duty of those who govern to those who are governed" would subject "the government to the just reproach of the world" (351). For Marshall, responsibility, duty, and obligation were not relics of a bygone era. On the contrary, these terms applied to economic as well as political actors in the legitimate functions they exercised over the nation's economic affairs.

Yet Marshall's classical republicanism in *Ogden* looked beyond posi-tive law as a sanction for enforcing contracts. The formation of agreements of exchange reflected and depended on a basic trust among the parties that drew up a contract, a trust that arose not from the specter of state enforcement but from mutual and informal expectations of performance. This moral dimension of contracts did not simply disappear with the state of nature, and ultimately its observance rested on civic rather than legal foundations. As Marshall allowed, "all admit that the Constitution refers to and preserves the legal, not the moral, obligation of a contract" (25 U.S. 337). The long-term survival of economic arrangements was built on the informal relationships created by citizens, those that were "enforced by the operation of internal and invisible agents, not by the agency of human laws" (338). Notwithstanding his unwavering veneration of the Constitution, Marshall recognized the importance of civil society, an area characterized by the willingness of citizens to keep their word with each another. He understood that a stable economy was built on and included communities of citizens, not independent actors. Financial prosperity went hand in hand with civic prosperity, and for Marshall these two types of flourishing related to each other in ways that were often diminished by the rule of profit maximization.

On few occasions were Marshall's liberal and republican credentials more clearly articulated than in *Ogden*. Yet in the course of discussing these concepts, he also identified a different kind of republicanism, one based on principles he saw endangered by the consequences of the Court's decision. Other scholars have labeled the idea using such various terms as neo-republicanism or "non-domination." But for Marshall, the Constitution, not an abstract neo-republican liberty, was the nation's foremost guard against political domination. Turning to this element of his political thought, we can understand Marshall's dissent as looking backward and forward in time, explaining themes that guided the creation of the Constitution while also issuing a warning of dangers that lurked on the near horizon.

Marshall's Constitutional Republicanism

Although Marshall was indebted to the traditions of republicanism and liberalism inherited by his generation, he was creative in how he interwove them. While liberalism and republicanism may have been the most prominent political philosophies in early American political culture, these traditions were in flux. As John Gunnell insists, "the much contested issue of the philosophy of the founding" is best resolved by leaving behind "the fundamental premise . . . that there was a distinct, or dominant, philosophy."[33] Throughout the eighteenth century, North America was undergoing a transition from a premodern to a modern social and political order, and prevailing understandings of republicanism were not exempt from this change.[34] Yet however at odds the core components of liberalism and republicanism were up to this time, the two philosophies often merged during this period in American history, particularly in the writings and oratory of the Jeffersonians.[35] In this regard, many scholars have identified during these years the emergence of a new "commercial republicanism," a theory that wedded classical liberalism's stress on private interest to republican concerns for the common welfare.[36] Thinkers as diverse as Adam Smith, Montesquieu, Benjamin Franklin, and Alexis de Tocqueville held to a common conviction that a society based on interdependence fostered by commercial exchanges would admit "a more sensible and realizable alternative" to ancient republics that were sustained by small, homogenous populations governed by civic virtue or divine law.[37] As Thomas Pangle concludes, this distinctly modern vision of republicanism reflected the American tendency to pine after "compromising formulations" of liberalism and republicanism that "would enable them to incorporate or exploit the classical and biblical heritages as apparent precursors, or comfortable allies, of modern natural-rights theory."[38]

More recently, a new approach championed mainly by Quentin Skinner and Philip Pettit has posited a similar theory of republican liberty, characterized by what they call "non-domination."[39] In contrast to those who would drive a hard distinction between positive liberty defined as self-determination and negative liberty characterized as freedom from interference, such neo-republicans argue for a third way.[40] For these authors, liberty does not consist of simply being able to manage one's affairs free from the active interference of an external authority. Freedom is complex: it is neither "positive" nor "negative."[41] Rather, liberty is only truly realized in the absence of the prospect of arbitrary political interference, now or in the future.[42] Legal barriers must guard against an individual's dependence on the will—even the goodwill—of some higher political power.[43] This understanding of liberty, Pettit argues, was recovered in the modern era as a new form of republicanism, one possessing "a juridical cast in which a central place was given to the notion of rights—customary, legal, and constitutional rights—as bulwarks against absolute power."[44] On this understanding, as he recently put it, to be free is to be "secure against any master in the domain of basic liberties," to be "safeguarded against the *dominatio* or domination of others," and to be "adequately and equally guarded by the law."[45] Perhaps, moreover, it shows how liberalism and republicanism might be complementary rather than antagonistic traditions.[46] But above all, neo-republicanism represents a theory that is neither wholly liberal nor republican. Rather, it borrows elements from both theories to advance a hybrid type of liberty.

This was the kind of liberty Marshall expounded in his *Ogden* dissent.[47] He too was apprehensive of sources of political domination. And, like modern neo-republicans, he emphasized the rule of law as an essential guard against potential incursions on liberty. Yet, given his devotion to the Constitution's legitimacy and sovereignty, we can more precisely classify Marshall's argument as that of a constitutional republican, one committed to preserving the common good and individual liberty alike within the framework of the nation's fundamental law. Wary of the dangers of political domination, his theory hews more closely to the security found in the nuts and bolts, the clauses and provisions, and the overall predictability and transparency of the Constitution.

Given his previous shootout with the Maryland legislature and its Virginia defenders in *McCulloch*, it is little wonder that Marshall feared domination emanating from the state governments. The New York statute was no legitimate interference in private contractual relationships, such as requirements that "certain agreements shall be in writing, that they shall be sealed, [or] that they shall be attested by a certain number of witnesses" (25 U.S. 348). Here was an act that went further, affecting all future contractual relationships in a way that could "seldom be justified" (334). It was "a very unusual and a very extraordinary exercise of the legislative power," a marked departure from legislation that acted "externally" on economic matters or even laws that governed the formalities of future contracts (343, 344). Its stipulations operated "on a future, contingent, unforeseen event," suspending the "impairing faculty" of the law until it might be exercised on those instances of insolvency that are "possible" but "never expected." It was no exaggeration to say that the statute represented an invasion of private agreements, inserting a provision that became a "constituent" part of existing agreements (339). The statute anticipated default, planned for its occurrence, and took no heed of the general consequences of these assumptions for the economic as well as political order.

In Marshall's view, the New York law went further than violating private agreements and nullifying the intrinsic obligation of contracts. Equally dangerous was the fact that it undermined one of the Constitution's greatest legal barriers to arbitrary government. The contract clause is found in the first paragraph of Section 10, a paragraph that "contains an enumeration of those cases in which the action of the state legislature is entirely prohibited" (25 U.S. 334). Such prohibitions are absolute and unequivocal, encompassing legislative acts "affecting the rights of individuals." When the framers forbade states from coining their own money, issuing bills of attainder, enacting ex post facto laws, or granting titles of nobility, Marshall argued, they were protecting individual liberty. Restrictions on the types of currency used to pay debts and the ban on state impairment of contracts were written with an eye to "legislative interference with private rights" and had been plainly devised to "restrain that interference" (336). And, Marshall insisted, nowhere did individual liberty find a surer protection from the legislatures than in the provision banning state laws impairing the obligation of contracts. The language of the clause makes the prohibition "complete and total. There is no exception from it. Legislation of every description is comprehended within it" (335).

Marshall's dissent was concerned with more than parsing the constitutionality of the statute and repudiating the easy positivism advanced by defenders of the law, who suggested that contract was the mere "creature of society," deriving "its obligation from the law" under which it is enacted (25 U.S. 344). Of even greater alarm was the threat to liberty forecast by its provisions. Viewed in isolation, the statute seemed to be small potatoes. But extend the principles implicit in the Court's explanation, and there was no telling where the state's power over the liberty of citizens might end. Thus the consequences of upholding the statute reached far beyond insolvency law, far beyond the state of New York. Marshall feared the ripple effects of such reasoning, or, as he put it, the "enormity" of the principle at hand (339). Carry the law to its logical conclusion, and all matters of contractual agreement were beholden to the whims of the state legislatures. Perhaps lawmakers might not take the implications of their policies so far. But for Marshall, as for many neo-republicans, the mere prospect of legislative domination over the contract rights of individuals was what counted.[48] His point related not to whether the legislature *would* interfere in contracts the future, but that it *could*. The "idea" behind the legislation, Marshall explained, must be brought to light and its implications "pressed still further" in order to open individuals' eyes to its full effects. At bottom, such legislation substituted the judgment of politicians for the liberty of individuals. Authorize the legislature to take upon itself this authority now, he warned, and the freedom to contract would henceforth be placed in an uncertain and vulnerable position indeed. "If one law enters into all subsequent contracts," he observed, "so does every other law which relates to the subject." Imagine a legislative act "declaring that all contracts should be subject to legislative control and should be discharged as the legislature might prescribe." If this scenario were to come to pass—if the legislative will were to encompass each "component part of every contract"—would any parties dare draw up long-term agreements? In Marshall's estimate, there was no turning back: introducing into a contract a single stipulation "not admitted by the parties" may in due course lead to the absolute dominion of politicians over citizens' economic transactions and affairs. Henceforth, he prophesied, ever changing popular opinion and the rise and fall of political parties would determine the legitimacy of contracts. The pleasure of the state legislatures, not the impartial rule of law, would regulate individuals' economic affairs.

As much as individual liberty was endangered by the state law, the nation's civic health was also in jeopardy. Marshall recognized that legal decisions resonated throughout society, not merely among the nation's financial elite. For him, freedom for all citizens was at stake. By assuming for itself "the power of changing the relative situation of debtor and creditor, of interfering with contracts," the legislature had jeopardized a freedom that went "home to every man" (25 U.S. 354). Such legislation not only affected the marketplace, but also "touches the interest of all, and controls the conduct of every individual in those things which he supposes to be proper for his own exclusive management" (354–55). No individual, Marshall believed, could be fully free so long as legislatures acted on the rights of individuals based on their own whims (355). Here was "a course of legislation which must end in self-destruction," a brazen seizure of power (353). Upholding the New York statute was bad enough, but even worse was that the Court had acquiesced to the possibility of further abuses of liberty going forward.

Moving beyond the particulars of the case at hand, Marshall trained his fire on more threats than those posed by the state governments. Throughout *Ogden*, Marshall gestures toward the specter of political domination as issuing from any number of directions. As a general matter, he emphasized, citizens must be vigilant of their freedoms. Liberty of contract was endangered wherever an individual's choices depended not on "the stipulations an individual makes," but on "some declaration of the supreme power of a state to which he belongs" (25 U.S. 344). Arbitrary authority could clothe itself in a variety of forms, whether that of legislatures, popular majorities, or even the domination asserted by one nation over another. But regardless of the particular manifestation of such power, its exercise was "an abuse of power which could scarcely be misunderstood" as long as it was deployed wantonly and without regard to the liberty of others (352). As he put it, the "rightfulness of coercion" depends not on the "superior strength" of a party, which rests on no higher authority than the rule of the strongest (345). Coercive force could only be justified by a "preexisting obligation to do that for which compulsion is used." That is to say, absent the state of nature, compulsion could only be safely carried out in conformity to the rule of law as inscribed in the Constitution.[49] Any assertion of authority disregarding its binding force, whether by elected officials or an unelected tribunal, was autocratic. Might did not make right.

Like many neo-republicans, Marshall emphasized the importance of political institutions and the rule of law as imposing a necessary bar on the possibility of political domination. A great defender of individual liberty and even (as in *Marbury*) popular sovereignty, he was also cautious about democratic decision making.[50] In his view, one need not look too far into the nation's history for an example of the effects of unchecked legislative authority. Under the Articles of Confederation, Marshall recalled, commercial intercourse and the existence of credit were wrecked by the states. Indeed, the neglect of debt payment and other debtors' relief laws were a "mischief" carried on "to such an excess" by the state governments as to "break in upon the ordinary intercourse of society" (25 U.S. 355). Marshall minced no words: the arbitrary course of state legislation had eroded "confidence between man and man." Indeed, more than undermining "the existence of credit and the sanctity of private faith," political meddling had sapped the very "morals of the people." No wonder an imposition of legal restraint on state legislation "was thought necessary by all those patriots who could take an enlightened and comprehensive view of our situation," even while disagreement was rife concerning the "various schemes of government" proposed in Philadelphia. Thus the clear and unambiguous language of the contract clause was included in the Constitution they proposed, whose restrictive language indicated "perpetuity," not a provision that "every state in the Union may elude at pleasure." Siding with state legislation against the law of the Constitution meant exchanging the solid security of constitutional government for the passions of the moment and the disjointed, unpredictable policies of local politicians.

The most effective curb to political domination rested in the Constitution, which provided the legal structure and protections necessary to thwart invasions of liberty by elected branches of the states and national government. For Marshall, both liberals and republicans neglected at their peril the importance of its rule. It was the Constitution that guaranteed rights and obligations while also standing against threats to both of these objects. But absent a reasonable approach to interpreting such provisions as the contract clause, textual bulwarks would exert little practical force. In *Ogden*, Marshall dwells on his own philosophy of constitutional interpretation in considerable detail, holding that above all "the intention of the instrument must prevail," based on its words "understood in that sense in which they are generally used by those for whom the instrument was intended" (25 U.S. 332). As he did in *McCulloch*, he emphasized once again that the document's "provisions are neither to be restricted into insignificance, nor extended to objects not comprehended in them, nor contemplated by its framers." For Marshall, the neo-republican emphasis on legal protections amounted to little if the Constitution's words were either shrunk into impotence or tortured and enlarged beyond their historical understanding.

Yet if the Constitution contained stipulations preserving individual liberty, Marshall believed the document also included silences that warranted judicial deference. Ever the defender of a more powerful national government, he nonetheless understood that even its reach should have limits. Especially in matters of economic liberty, Marshall believed that the document wisely recognized that a "great mass of human transactions" arose informally among individuals (25 U.S. 341). Thus the framers drafted a document that would facilitate rather than frustrate the nation's commercial progress. In particular, the meaning of its contract clause was absolute, unequivocal, and final: "No State," it declared, "shall . . . pass any . . . Law impairing the Obligation of Contracts." Thus the document's language called for "restraint as to the obligation of contracts," not a ready "hostility to invade the inviolability of contract, which is placed beyond its reach" (351–52). Its words treated citizens and state governments alike with a language of respect as befitting "intelligent beings understanding their duties and willing to perform them; not as insane beings who must be compelled to act for self-preservation" (351).[51] In brief, the Constitution secured for citizens their freedom to deliberate, plan, set terms, and fulfill the agreements they reached with one another. More than national political officials, the state governments, or even the judiciary, it was the Constitution that provided to the American people a fence against political domination.

Conclusions

Political domination was an enduring concern for Marshall during his tenure on the Supreme Court. It is a theme that is found in several of his opinions both before and after his dissent in *Ogden* and was invoked in a wider context than debtor relief laws. As we have already seen, in *Marbury* he did not flinch from defending a citizen's right to the minor position of Justice of the Peace. In *Ex parte Bollman, Ex parte Swartwout* (1807), and his supervision of the conspiracy trial of Aaron Burr, he stood up for the rights of the accused in ordering the discharge of individuals detained under charges of treason.[52] In *Gibbons v. Ogden* (1824), his opinion struck the fatal blow to the powerful Livingston-Fulton coasting monopoly.[53] And as we shall see in the next chapter, in his opinions in *Cherokee Nation v. Georgia* (1831) and *Worcester v. Georgia* (1832), he set his face against federal and state governments alike in vindicating the self-government rights of the Native American tribes. Pursuing Marshall's argument in *Ogden* should point us to connecting political domination discussed there to these other, more familiar opinions. But only in the *Ogden* dissent do we find his most candid and coherent statement of the threat posed by political domination. Moreover, it is in this opinion, when Marshall wrote on behalf of his own views rather than those of the Court, that we arrive at a complete understanding of the nexus between liberalism and republicanism that informed his political thought.

   For Marshall, *Ogden v. Saunders* involved grander issues than bankruptcy law, contractual performance, or even the more typical questions the Supreme Court confronted concerning federal versus state sovereignty. On a larger scale, the case affected society "deeply and seriously," revolving around fundamental tensions involving economic versus political authority, individual rights in the state of nature, and the claims of civil society (25 U.S. 338). While Marshall was clearly disturbed by the economic consequences of New York's newfound influence over economic affairs, something greater than a hardboiled libertarian ideology characterized his dissent in the case. An anxiety permeates the dissent, perhaps reflecting the fact that by this point in his tenure, a number of Marshall's core beliefs were under fire. Not only were rights increasingly threatened, but republican virtues of duty and obligation were also at a low point. The doctrine of states' rights was once again rearing its head. And looming on the national horizon was the prospect of uncontrolled state legislatures, now possessing the Court's imprimatur to wield unprecedented power over the national economy. In many ways, Marshall's dissent represents an effort to slow the crisis toward which he believed the nation was hurtling.

Seen in this light, the *Ogden* dissent is significant not simply for its status as the single occasion when Marshall departed from the consensus and unity he sought so diligently to build as Chief Justice. Nor is his dissent simply another testament of his skeptical view of the state legislatures. On this occasion, Marshall spoke the language of liberal natural rights as well as that of classical republican duty and obligation to build his argument against the majority opinion. But despite his support for elements of both theories, he does not limit himself to these two frameworks. Beyond liberalism and republicanism was Marshall's understanding of the special danger posed by arbitrary authority in the United States. Such dangers were made plain in the extra-constitutional acts of political officials, but were also lurking wherever liberties were put at risk. While vigilance might guard against these dangers, for Marshall something more was needed. The nation's greatest security, he believed, was found in a more concrete object: the iron law of the Constitution.

Finally, *Ogden* pushes back against theories of neo-republicanism that would minimize the dangers political domination poses to economic liberty. Like many contemporary neo-republicans, Marshall saw liberalism and republicanism in complementary terms as theories that are united against the dangers of political domination. But unlike many of them, he also emphasizes economic rights as important dimensions of individual liberty. Neo-republicans rightfully pay careful attention to power inequalities in society, seeking to correct theories of freedom that have privileged "the sector of interest and opinion that first gave [them] prominence and currency."[54] In doing so, they seek to highlight sources of domination (notably by socioeconomic elites) that they dubiously claim have received little notice.[55] Nonetheless, Philip Pettit himself has recently admitted that the enjoyment of basic liberties requires in part the freedom "to associate and incorporate with one another on a suitable contractual basis."[56] Without denying that domination can indeed issue from the economic relationships, Marshall reminds readers that state interference may jeopardize economic freedoms along with other types of individual liberties.[57] Neo-republican theory must continue to grapple with the challenge raised by *Ogden*, with careful attention given to the breadth of economic regulation within a nation committed to republican freedom.[58]

Not to be lost in this discussion of markets is Marshall's political thought. Drawing on the influence of classical liberal and republican principles for understanding contractual obligation, Marshall pressed beyond these traditions to recognize the institutions of law to engage the concept of domination as a political thinker whose creed was neither uniformly liberal nor republican. In its concern for individual rights and duty, *Ogden* bears the imprint of the classical liberal and republican traditions that held sway during the founding era. Yet at the center of the prevailing theories of Marshall's day lived a republicanism of his own, one that rested on his defense of the Constitution against threats to liberty. Though he was in the unfamiliar position of being on the losing side in *Ogden*, he was correct to remain on his guard against the state legislatures. As he would soon discover, his greatest reckoning with the states was yet to come.

4

The Native American Trilogy and the
Idea of Constitutional Nationalism

Addressing themes of legitimacy, sovereignty, and republicanism, the common thread of *Marbury v. Madison, McCulloch v. Maryland,* and *Ogden v. Saunders* is their application to white citizens of the United States. To complete our analysis of Marshall's political thought, however, it is necessary to shift its application to those who in his day fell outside the parameters of citizenship. The Native American cases comprising the so-called Marshall Trilogy—*Johnson v. M'Intosh* (1823), *Cherokee Nation v. Georgia* (1831), and *Worcester v. Georgia* (1832)—provided the occasion for the Chief Justice to do so. On this occasion, Marshall did more than mediate the perennial dispute between state authority and tribal sovereignty. He also presented a constitution-based national identity, and in doing so articulated the Constitution's embrace of all Americans.

The Trilogy capped a wretched chapter in American history. Beginning in the 1820s, the Supreme Court of the United States began considering various claims of sovereignty by American Indian tribes in the midwestern and southern United States, particularly those living in the state of Georgia.[1] With the stroke of Marshall's pen, the Court's three major Native American opinions effectively shut the door of the Court to Cherokee and other tribal land claims. In spite of Marshall's clear opposition to the state policies authorizing forced migration and his open contempt for President Andrew Jackson's indifference toward the plight of the Native American tribes, his opinions in the three cases made clear that there was little he could do apart from reminding the elected branches of their duties. "If it be true that the Cherokee Nation have rights, this is not the tribunal in which those rights are to be asserted," he concluded in *Cherokee Nation v. Georgia* (30 U.S. 20). "If it be true that wrongs have been inflicted, and that still greater are to be apprehended, this is not the tribunal which can redress the past or prevent the future." For the representatives of the Indian nations who had brought their claims before the Court, Marshall's principled defense of tribal sovereignty was cold comfort.

Marshall scholars have long seen the outcome of the Marshall Trilogy as a failure on the part of the Chief Justice, although some have portrayed it as an honorable one.[2] After all, they argue, because congressional Democrats were firmly in lockstep with President Jackson's commitment to state sovereignty, the removal of the tribes was a fait accompli even before their cause reached the Court. As Charles Hobson puts it, these cases "underscored the judiciary's impotence in the face of a determined political majority," illustrating its status as the weakest branch of the national government.[3] Even those who otherwise praise the Marshall Court acknowledge that Jackson's famous (though likely apocryphal) quip in response to the holding in *Worcester*—"John Marshall has made his decision; now let him enforce it!"[4]—put the exclamation point on a stinging defeat for Marshall, the "consummate judicial politician" whose Court rarely looked so hamstrung and helpless.[5] To be sure, some scholars have argued that Marshall's dialogue with the political branches deserves more attention than it has received.[6] And a few have noted the importance of Marshall's elaboration of principles of tribal sovereignty for understanding the foundations of federal Indian law.[7] But whether the result of party politics, hardwired institutional constraints, or a combination of the two, the verdicts delivered a uniform message: neither Marshall nor his Court would give any immediate help to the tribes.

Yet if Marshall was aware of the headwinds blowing against the Court, he did not flinch from defending the tribes, invalidating state acts that had been passed to limit their rights when given the opportunity, and upholding the law of the Constitution that protected them both consistently and repeatedly. Aware that there was nothing his Court could do to avert Native American removal, he nonetheless refused to ignore the crisis facing the tribes. Nor was his broader message limited to Native Americans. As he did in the other opinions we have examined, Marshall's words in these cases makes clear his intention to use the opportunity to convey a larger message—to the American Indian tribes, to supporters of their removal, and, indeed, to all Americans.[8] For the Trilogy addressed at its core the Constitution's implications not only for the land and political rights of Native Americans, but also for the relationship between federal and state authority, a topic that would become volatile with the passage of South Carolina's Nullification Ordinance only months after *Worcester* was decided.[9] Indeed, as in *Marbury*, *McCulloch*, and *Ogden*, the Marshall Trilogy would address questions of constitutional and political theory that would loom large throughout the antebellum period and beyond. Unlike the *Ogden* dissent, however, the importance of the Trilogy has not gone unnoticed by Marshall scholars. Robert Faulkner argues that the Native American cases stand out for Marshall's careful treatment of the "tension between natural liberty and civil government."[10] Richard Brisbin sees the extensive use of early American political history in these cases as a calculated effort to restore confidence in the virtues of national authority at a moment when fears of centralization ran high.[11] More recently, Supreme Court Justice Stephen Breyer has suggested that the cases demonstrate Marshall's command of a variety of political concepts in navigating the Court's "collision between law and morality on the one hand, and desire and force on the other."[12] But beyond these appraisals, Marshall's thinking in these cases shows his abiding concern with the development of a strong sense of national identity in the still new but rapidly expanding United States. For Marshall, responding to this concern began and ended with the Constitution.

Nevertheless, Marshall's views concerning American nationalism in these opinions have remained largely unexplored. In truth, he approached these questions carefully, being well aware that nationalism was a Janus-faced force that was at once liberating and oppressive, potentially promoting freedom and social cohesion, but also possibly encouraging intolerance and mob rule.[13] Thus, in identifying sources of American nationalism, he acknowledged the powerful attractions of ethnic ties and universal principles. In the end, however, he settled on a theory of nationalism entirely his own. Given what we know of Marshall's political thought so far, the fact that he would turn to the Constitution as an alternative approach to nationalism is unsurprising. What is remarkable, however, is his belief that the document could do more for the American people than fashion a legal order protecting rights, establishing uniform laws, and promoting economic growth. Marshall's constitutional nationalism as it emerged from these opinions may not have resonated much in his own time, but its aims are crucial for understanding the implications of his thought for nations that continue to struggle with the possibilities and perils of nationalism today.

The Native American Cases Revisited

The Court's first major decision concerning Native American land owner-ship, *Johnson v. M'Intosh* (1823), did not bode well for the tribes.[14] Here was a case whose outcome bore directly on their future, yet neither party was Native American![15] The dispute related to a 1775 purchase of land in present-day Illinois from the Piankeshaw Indians by a number of colonists, including former Supreme Court Justice Thomas Johnson. Following the Revolutionary War, the Piankeshaw sold the previously purchased parcel of land to the federal government, of which 10,000 acres were later pur-chased by William McIntosh, a prominent real estate entrepreneur and fur trader.[16] In response, Johnson's heirs sued to establish their title to the land as anterior to and thus invalidating the later purchase by McIntosh.

In deciding the case, the Court confronted the questions of whether land grants issued by the tribes were reviewable by federal courts and, generally, whether Native Americans possessed the power to purchase and sell titles to their land to private buyers. Marshall's opinion would deliver a victory not only to McIntosh, but also to the federal government, while firmly establishing what the opinion deemed "the right of society to prescribe those rules by which property may be acquired and preserved" (21 U.S. 572). According to Marshall, the validity of land titles depended not on considerations of natural law or justice, but on the positive law of the land in which territory resided. Prior to the American Revolution, he asserted, the British gained title and possession to North American land through discovery, a rule "the great nations of Europe"—British, French, Spanish, and other nation-states—acknowledged in order to peacefully settle land claims during their shared exploration of North America.[17] According to the Treaty of Paris, Great Britain relinquished to the states not only claims over government, but titles pertaining to the "propriety and territorial rights of the United States" (584). To be sure, Native Americans remained "rightful occupants of the soil, with a legal as well as just claim to retain possession of it" (574). Yet the doctrine of discovery as expounded by Marshall ensured that "their rights to complete sovereignty as indepen-dent nations," in his words, "were necessarily diminished." Of particular relevance to Johnson's heirs, the right of Native Americans "to dispose of the soil at their own will to whomsoever they pleased" was superseded by the sovereignty of the federal government and the commerce clause, which prohibited the sale of tribal lands by Native Americans to private citizens. Indeed, as Marshall put it, it was a "broad principle which had always been maintained that the exclusive right to purchase from the Indians resided in the government" (585). The validity of McIntosh's title was confirmed, but more portentous for the Native Americans was the distinction Marshall had drawn between land occupation and ownership. As Marshall put it, to confuse the two concepts, or worse yet to conflate them, would call into question the validity of all non-Native land titles. Indeed, it would cast doubt on the legitimacy of the national government itself, an implication he strenuously avoided. In short, with *Johnson*, Native Americans became occupants, not owners of land.

What are we to make of Marshall's discovery doctrine as expounded in *Johnson*? Given what we already know about him, the opinion was not his most coherent work. On this occasion, his longtime defense of property rights clashed with his skepticism toward Native American land titles, resulting in the rather convoluted theory of quasi-tribal sovereignty. Yet the discovery doctrine was not invented out of thin air by Marshall. In fact, its origins are traceable to Christian efforts to subjugate non-Christian lands, such as papal bulls issued during the Inquisition centuries earlier.[18] Nonetheless, *Johnson* has remained a source of intense controversy in the eyes of scholars of Native American history and federal Indian law, with some convinced that a power play was at work in Marshall's opinion. Stuart Banner, for example, has argued that in fact the English government's land policy typically "treated the Indians as owners of the land" and because land was abundant and usually cheap, it made more sense to placate Native Americans by purchasing their land rather than seizing it.[19] In light of this possibility, Lindsay Robertson speculates that Marshall introduced the discovery doctrine to guarantee the land rights of war veterans who had received land grants in Virginia's western territory prior to the American Revolution. Such titles had not been ceded to the United States and were not validated until an act of Congress in 1830.[20] Regardless of Marshall's motives in *Johnson*—whether he aimed at a faithful history of the relations between whites and Native Americans or sought to shore up the existing land claims of his fellow Virginians—the right of discovery and limited ownership became the cornerstones of federal Indian law, even influencing the definition of indigenous land rights worldwide.[21]

The discovery doctrine did not occupy pride of place in *Cherokee Nation v. Georgia* (1831), but territorial claims now loomed even larger over the United States. Throughout the eighteenth and nineteenth centuries, the national government eagerly purchased lands the Cherokee were willing to sell, often relying on less than aboveboard means.[22] Over time, the territory held by the tribes eroded as sales to the federal government grew. All the while, the Cherokee Nation remained on good diplomatic terms with the federal government, even as national officials began to bow to non-Native demands for tribal land in the name of state sovereignty. The relationship reached a critical pass in the early 1800s: the government found itself in a bind, having consistently made promises to the Cherokee that their title to unsold land was secure while also pledging their removal to western territory to placate state governments.[23] By the 1820s, the heat on national officials was turned up by the states yet again as the discovery of gold in Georgia and an increased demand for land due to population growth demanded that some resolution—a forcible one, if necessary—be brought to the status of the Native American tribes.[24]

The Cherokee, however, had other plans. What little of their ancestral land remained was precious: they wished to continue living in Georgia and were understandably reluctant to be exiled to the wild western territory. To overcome this resistance, in 1824 the state legislature began passing a number of measures designed to force Native Americans from the state. The acts represented a sharp rupture in an increasingly strained relationship between Georgia and the Cherokee, culminating with an act proclaiming that after June 1, 1830, all Cherokee customs, laws, and ordinances were entirely void and its territory subject to such regulations the state might issue. Tribal sovereignty was quickly eroding—indeed, already appeared to be eroded entirely—and there was little that could be done politically to prevent it. Turned away by President Jackson, who supported removal along with Congress, Chief John Ross turned to the able counsel of former Attorney General William Wirt and took the Cherokee case to the Supreme Court. Requesting a federal injunction to restrain ordinances that, if allowed to stand, would in their view "go directly to annihilate the Cherokees as a political society," the tribe filed suit as a foreign nation under the Court's original jurisdiction (30 U.S. 15).

The advocates for the Cherokee Nation had some reason to expect a more sympathetic hearing from the Supreme Court. In fact, it was Marshall's dicta in the often reviled *Johnson v. M'Intosh*, the decision that one scholar has recently claimed "hollowed out the core of Indian sovereignty," that the Cherokee looked to with hope.[25] In *Cherokee Nation v. Georgia*, the issue was not land sales but internal governance, and Marshall had clearly emphasized in *Johnson* that Native Americans enjoyed self-rule in land they had not transferred or sold to the federal government.[26] Nevertheless, in *Cherokee Nation*, the Court was little help to the tribes, ruling that it in fact lacked jurisdiction to hear the case. The reason had to do with the legal standing of the Cherokee Nation under Article III. The Cherokee had argued that their controversy fell under the Court's original jurisdiction involving suits between two or more states or between a state and a foreign nation. Marshall disagreed. The Constitution's categorization of the Indian Tribes as separate from the several states and foreign nations, particularly in the language of the commerce clause, doomed their standing, and Marshall held that the Native Americans could not maintain an action against the state of Georgia (30 U.S. 17). Neither a state nor an independent nation in the eyes of the Court—"domestic dependent nations," rather—the Cherokee stood by helplessly as the Court declined to issue an injunction against Georgia's policies. In articulating this gray zone, a subtle shift in tone seemed to have occurred in the Court's attitude toward Native Americans. A certain patronization creeps into Marshall's writing. If he still held to his statements in *Johnson*—that the Native Americans were practically coequal negotiating partners with the United States government and that their internal sovereignty remained inviolate—on this occasion he would not stand by those words.

That would soon change. In the final case of the Trilogy, *Worcester v. Georgia* (1832), the Court again confronted state laws interfering with the internal sovereignty of the Cherokee. Yet on this occasion, the injured parties were both Native Americans and non-Native American citizens. In 1825, Vermont minister Samuel Worcester led a group of missionaries to the Cherokee territory, preaching Christianity while also organizing a successful printing press and newspaper. Worcester's mission ran afoul of Georgia's 1830 regulations of the Cherokee, which included provisions requiring all white men living on Native American land to procure a state license and swear an oath to uphold Georgia laws while residing within the boundaries of the Cherokee Nation. Worcester and several other missionaries refused the oath—he instead mailed the governor a hymnbook—and were summarily arrested, tried, convicted, and sentenced to four years of hard labor. Although several of the prisoners received pardons, Worcester was one of the few who refused one so that a suit might be brought before the Supreme Court.

In a 5–1 decision, the Court struck down Worcester's conviction. Citing several treaties negotiated between the federal government and the Cherokee Nation, Marshall held that the Georgia acts were in violation of Article VI's supremacy clause. Renewing a theme introduced in *Johnson*, Marshall declared that the United States government had long considered the Native Americans as "distinct, independent political communities retaining their original natural rights," and there were no legal grounds for the Georgia legislature's interference in tribal lands in light of the Native Americans' legitimate title to their territory (31 U.S. 519). Moreover, given that Worcester and his fellow missionaries were visiting the Cherokee in pursuit of federal laws promoting "the humane policy of the Government of the United States, for the civilization and improvement of the Indians," there was also no legal basis for their arrest or punishment by state authorities (529). Put simply, "under colour of a law which is void, as being repugnant to the Constitution, treaties, and laws of the United States," the courts of Georgia had upheld the imprisonment of Worcester and his fellow missionaries (562). Hence their convictions, Marshall concluded in no uncertain terms, should be summarily rescinded (563).

To the dismay—if not the surprise—of the Cherokee leadership, Marshall's words had no direct impact. The immediate disregard of the Court's verdicts by Georgia drowned out Marshall's defense of the Cherokee. Georgia had not even deigned to send a lawyer to defend its position before the Court. It is true that the decision may have inspired some federal action on behalf of the imprisoned missionaries, forcing a reluctant president's hand to adopt a tougher stance on behalf of federal law in the face of state nullification laws.[27] The Cherokee, however, obtained a hollow victory. Following *Worcester*, infighting would erupt among the Cherokee on whether to leave Georgia or remain there in the hope that further negotiations with state officials might forestall the land grab. But Jackson's reelection in 1832 suggested that removal was inevitable. Three years later, a faction of the Cherokee overcame fierce resistance within the tribe and signed a treaty of peaceable removal—the Treaty of New Echota—exchanging Georgia lands for those in western territory.[28]

The fate of the Marshall Trilogy has fared little better than the Cherokee. Though still required reading for students of American Indian law, the Trilogy continues to be often disregarded by members of the modern Supreme Court.[29] As a result, apart from a few infelicitous catchphrases— "domestic dependent nations" or "ward to his guardian"—Marshall's words in the cases are often remembered for what they were unable to effect rather than their positive impact. Yet we would do well to heed his argument on behalf of constitutional nationalism in these cases, for they resonate today in a way they did not in the 1830s. Individually, each case addresses concepts of nationalism prominent during the Jacksonian era. Together these cases bring to light views concerning how the Constitution might serve as a source of national identity for all who resided within the United States. That said, standing in the way of this idea were the stubborn distinctions drawn by ethnicity.

Ethnonationalism

Nationalism has long been viewed through the prism of ethnicity. For many, bonds of kinship and history both precede and trump all other sources of cultural identity. For those who hold this view, nationalism is not an airy abstraction or product of human design, but an innate and organic concept based on claims of blood or soil. Among recent scholars, Anthony Smith may have made the strongest case for this primordialist understanding of nationalism, arguing that national solidarities are fundamentally affective rather than rational and that they are rooted in distinct histories and ideologies traceable as far back as the Middle Ages.[30] National solidarity, in Smith's assessment, is tied not only to a specific territory but also to those customs, mythologies, and historical memories that make up the public culture of a specific people.[31] Following along the same lines, Walker Connor, a leading student of ethnonationalism, has claimed that a nation consists simply of "a group of people who believe they are ancestrally related."[32] According to Connor, nationalism represents "the largest group that can command a person's loyalty because of felt kinship ties; it is, from this perspective, the fully extended family."[33] For better or worse, these ancestral foundations of nationalism have proven surprisingly resilient in the age of globalization, with ethnic loyalties supplying a source of stability and continuity in times of change.[34] Thus scholars such as Cynthia Enloe, Donald Horowitz, Craig Calhoun, and Pierre Manent have all underlined the persistence of ethnicity for understanding national identity and modern sources of state conflict.[35] Indeed, in part owing to recent global economic upheavals, it is no exaggeration to claim that ethnic nationalism today is on the rise, having experienced a new lease on life.[36]

The ethnic differences between Native and non-Native Americans were never far from Marshall's mind. As was the case with African-Americans, these distinctions provoked the Chief Justice's sympathy rather than his antagonism.[37] Thus his opinion in *Cherokee Nation* begins with a note of remorse for the situation of the Cherokee. Indeed, he confessed that no case was "better calculated to excite" the Court's sympathies than the plight of the Native Americans (30 U.S. 15). Marshall emphasized that the

Native nations had undergone a remarkable social transformation since the American Revolution. Instead of an emergence from subjection to liberty, like most Americans, the Cherokee had followed the opposite path from freedom to dependence. A people "once numerous, powerful, and truly independent," they encountered the first European explorers "in the quiet and uncontrolled possession of an ample domain" in North America. In a short amount of time, this indigenous independence gave way to the arts, arms, and "superior policy" of the colonists. Now, having sold most of their land, the tribe had petitioned the Supreme Court in order to preserve what remnant of territory the Cherokee still held for their "comfortable subsistence." European settlers had wrought a transformation in North America, harnessing and cultivating its natural resources to create a booming agricultural and manufacture economy. Yet *Cherokee Nation* shows that this success story came at a cost, and that the country's economic order had often ignored the crisis faced by a people whose own national identity—whose very existence—was now threatened with extinction.

Marshall next turned to the jurisdictional question the case posed for the Court, namely, whether the case could be decided as one between a state and a foreign nation. The Cherokee had earnestly defended their status as a "distinct political society, separated from others, capable of managing its own affairs and governing itself" (30 U.S. 16). Certainly, Marshall affirmed, there was some truth to their assertions of self-rule. The manifold treaties existing between Native American tribes and the government of the United States seemed to treat the Cherokee like a distinct society, recognizing them as a people exercising authority over questions of war and peace and domestic policy. This argument, in the opinion of the majority of the justices at least, had proven "completely successful."

Such characteristics notwithstanding, the Court held that the Cherokee Nation constituted a distinct state, not a foreign nation.[38] Topographically, Cherokee lands were not separated from the rest of the country by vast seas or territory, but bounded on all sides by the state of Georgia, a part of the United States. In Marshall's words, "all our maps, geographical treatises, histories, and laws" confirmed the observation (30 U.S. 17). Thus enclosed, these lands rested within "the jurisdictional limits of the United States." Furthermore, in the many treaties negotiated between the United States and the Cherokee Nation, the Cherokee frequently acknowledged the protection of the United States and gave the federal government exclusive authority to regulate its trade. Indeed, before the Constitution was ever ratified, the tribes had deputized representatives to send to the Confederation Congress

(16). Additionally, they had repeatedly looked to the federal government for security from invaders of their rights. Because the government had come to the Native Americans' defense with such "kindness and power," it should excite little comment that the tribes had occasionally addressed the President of the United States as their "Great Father" (17). Looking abroad, Marshall continued, American Indians were regarded by other nations as "so completely under the sovereignty and dominion of the United States" that outside attempts to meddle in their affairs would incur the wrath of the United States government, not the Native nations themselves (17–18).

Yet in spite of the guardianship afforded to the tribes by the national government, they did not possess the same standing as Georgia or any other state in the United States. For Marshall, there existed a wide gap between the Cherokee Nation and the rest of the country. "The condition of the Indians in relation to the United States," he stressed, "is perhaps unlike that of any other two people in existence," with "peculiar and cardinal distinctions" that set them apart from non-Native Americans (30 U.S. 16). Economic production, language, and culture combined to form a situation vis-à-vis the rest of the country that obtained nowhere else in the world. The tribes, as Marshall famously put it, "may, more correctly, perhaps, be denominated domestic dependent nations" in a state of "pupilage" (17). With the protection of the United States, the relationship between the tribes and the government was not like Georgia to the United States, but one that resembled that "of a ward to his guardian." The implications of such a tutelage were clear: just as a parent could reasonably dispose of the goods of a child, so too could the United States regulate commerce among the Native Americans "independent of their will, which must take effect in point of possession when their right of possession ceases."

There was one more distinction separating the tribes from the rest of the nation, a difference that weighed particularly heavy in the Chief Justice's mind. Beyond the recognized differences in culture, history, and economy, the Native nations simply were not acclimated to the same legal traditions and customs familiar to most Americans. When the Constitution was being drafted, Marshall noted, the "habits and usages" of the tribes "in their intercourse with their white neighbors" were considered by the framers, and their views on the matter were not to be ignored (30 U.S. 18). At the time, intertribal conflict was resolved not through the channels of the political process or courts of law. Instead, assertions of right were appealed "to the tomahawk or to the [central] government." Scant familiarity with written law, criminal procedure, and just punishment for crimes set the tribes apart from the colonists who had assimilated these principles living under British or American courts of law. Admittedly, Marshall acknowledged that the tribes had since made progress from this state of affairs. But clearly the estimate of "the Statesmen who framed the Constitution," who set them apart from foreign nations in the commerce clause, continued to carry some weight with him.

In a variety of ways, then, *Cherokee Nation* distinguished the tribes as a unique ethnic community: geographically within the United States, but possessing the rights of self-government relating to their own internal affairs. They were their own civilization, not part of the American nation. Yet the sum of their language, traditions, culture, and history sufficiently distinguished them as a community that deserved the nation's protection, not its recognition as an independent state. Marshall reaffirmed his description of the Native Americans in *Johnson*, but refused to take the altogether different step of classifying the tribes as a completely foreign nation. Thus absent legitimate standing on the part of the Native Americans, the Court could not issue a determination on the constitutionality of the Georgia laws—for the moment.

Liberal Nationalism

In contrast to ethnicity, liberalism has had a more complicated experience with nationalism. Liberal theorists such as Isaiah Berlin have protested against national identities based on blood and soil as promoting violence and intolerance.[39] Yet beginning in the 1980s, liberals once more turned to national identity as a means for unifying diverse groups with various ethnic and tribal loyalties. Indeed, liberal theorists such as Yael Tamir, Will Kymlicka, David Miller, and others heartily endorse a civic nationalism based on values of equality and fairness as instrumental to stability and civic cohesion.[40] Miller, for example, has noted the appeal of nationalism as a concept supplying "the wherewithal for a common culture against whose background people can make more individual decisions about how to lead their lives," fostering "the mutual understanding and trust that makes democratic citizenship possible."[41] To be sure, some have called attention to the difficulties of dissolving all ethnic distinctions into a universal liberal solution, even going so far as to conclude that the generality of liberalism and the particularity of nationalism are ultimately antagonistic.[42] Thus, to mitigate these dangers, contemporary scholars of liberal nationalism typically steer clear of static definitions, instead favoring an open-ended, contested, and plural articulation of national identity, one intended to support the fluidity of national membership.[43]

The Marshall Trilogy articulates many of these themes of mutual understanding and accommodation. Although we have noticed the troubling claims about the dependency and pupilage of the tribes under the federal government, Marshall's opinions in the cases included numerous references to the common humanity of Native and non-Native Americans. It was a hopeful, perhaps even Romantic portrayal of the history between Native and non-Native Americans. There is ugliness swept under the rug. Nonetheless, he genuinely believed that the tribes deserved protection, and this conviction would seem to inform whatever sanitization enters into his narrative. Given the opportunity to at last render a judgment on state interference in tribal affairs in *Worcester*, he portrayed the relationship between the political leaders of the tribes and the state governments as more of a working partnership rather than a strict hierarchy, characterized above all by respect. Moreover, this relationship was a national one, guided by treaties that were supreme to all state legislation. Reviewing the many agreements and treaties Worcester's attorneys had cited in claiming sovereign immunity from Georgia's laws, he also acknowledged that on matters of internal policy, the Cherokee Nation did indeed possess the right to "govern themselves and all persons who have settled within their territory," free from legislative interference (31 U.S. 538). The state legislatures had done serious violence to the principle of internal tribal sovereignty and deserved blame for damaging a long-standing relationship of mutual accommodation between the tribes and federal officials.

Understanding the working relationship between the tribes and national government meant appreciating the diversity implicit in the American experience. Consistent with liberal theories of nationalism, Marshall emphasized that there was no straightforward and linear story to American nationhood. Rather, there was a plurality of voices and experiences that defined the current makeup of the nation, not the least of those being the experience of the Native Americans. The case of *Worcester* involved not only the fate of European missionaries, but also the plight and livelihood of "a once numerous and powerful people" (31 U.S. 536). Looking back to the first settlement of North America, the "adventurous sons" who embarked from the shores of Europe had set upon a new land "in possession of a people who had made small progress in agriculture or manufactures" and survived principally on the basis of "war, hunting, and fishing" (543). Overwhelmed by their surroundings, the settlers were eager "to avoid bloody conflicts which might terminate disastrously to all," and so justified their claims to the land in such a manner that did not abrogate the land rights of the tribes. A soft form of subjection emerged almost imperceptibly, as Native territory came under the protection of the colonists through a process of negotiation rather than domination.[44]

Wisely, Marshall concluded, foreign powers avoided provoking the resentment of the "fierce and warlike" character of the tribes, instead forming alliances and even friendships with them (31 U.S. 546). Comparing this historical account with a series of proclamations and speeches issued by British authorities, Marshall declared that it was certain "that our history furnishes no example from the first settlement of the country" of any attempt made by Great Britain to interfere with tribal affairs except to keep out the agents of foreign powers that might manipulate them into foreign alliances (547). Nor did the Continental Congress overturn Great Britain's attitude toward the tribes. The Cherokee had fought alongside the British in the American Revolution, but thereafter treaties were signed that promised protection of their tribal lands, confined their trading activity to the United States, and even permitted the tribes congressional representation (551). Native tribes were inseparable from American history, and though the framers conceived of them as "distinct political communities, having territorial boundaries within which their authority is exclusive," they never considered that the terms of their protection could "imply the destruction of the protected," as Georgia had wantonly presumed (557, 552).

Georgia's actions threatened not simply federal treaties, but also the relationship between the tribes and the rest of the nation. Marshall had to tread carefully in describing this relationship, and admittedly the portrait he paints is not without some creative license. While this relationship was never entirely harmonious, he argued, at least both parties had hitherto been on respectful speaking terms with each other. The policies of the state government, however, seemed to treat the tribes as objects, as less than human, as obstacles that needed to be pushed westward. This approach jarred with those of the earliest European settlers, in Marshall's view, for in his estimate "it is difficult to comprehend the proposition that the inhabitants of either quarter of the globe could have rightful original claims of dominion over the inhabitants of the other, or over the lands they occupied" (31 U.S. 543). Accommodation was necessary given that the country was "too immense for any one" to fully grasp, and its then claimants "too powerful to submit to the exclusive or unreasonable pretensions of any single potentate." Thus recourse was made to diplomacy, not violence: it was the practice of the Crown, colonial, and national governments to treat the tribes as "capable of maintaining the relations of peace and war; of governing themselves under her protection; and she made treaties with them the obligation of which she acknowledged" (548–49).[45] Every object that might provoke hostility was assiduously avoided; every policy that might further improve relations was pursued. Indeed, in passing measures for the relief of suffering tribes, the journals of Congress reveal "an anxious desire to conciliate the Indian nations" and "the most strenuous exertions" to promote friendship and prevent hostility (549).

As Marshall points out, the language of the various treaties reached between the tribes and the federal government illustrated the respect government officials afforded the Native Americans. Hence, the Hopewell Treaty of 1785 stressed mutual forgiveness of "all offences or acts of hostilities," a hope for "a perpetual peace and friendship" between the contracting parties and all succeeding generations, and free passage for Americans through Native American territory (31 U.S. 549). Admittedly, the treaty included a provision giving the United States power to manage some tribal affairs. But such a grant was for external defense of the tribes—to prevent the meddling of foreign powers, for example—and it would be a perversion of the "necessary meaning" of the treaty's words and a gross departure from their usual construction to suggest that they justified a surrender of their self-government (554). Next, Marshall looked to the treaty of Holston, negotiated in July 1791, which was designed to establish a more "solid peace" following the ratification of the Constitution. There, too, "the mutual desire of establishing permanent peace and friendship, and of removing all causes of war is honestly avowed" in express terms (555). Protection of the tribes is again mentioned, but for the narrow purposes of regulating trade and repelling "lawless and injurious intrusions," intrusions of the sort Georgia now seemed to be engaged in.

To Marshall, the policy of the federal government toward the tribes was clear. The 1819 Act of Congress promoting Native American civilization was intended to preserve the tribes, providing "against the further decline and final extinction of the Indian tribes," in its words (31 U.S. 557). Instruction and education in agriculture, writing, and arithmetic would be carried out only with tribal consent, which had been given. The Court's verdict necessarily followed: "The act of the State of Georgia, under which the plaintiff in error was prosecuted, is consequently void, and the judgment a nullity" (561). The conviction of the missionaries and the judgments upholding their sentences "ought, therefore, to be reversed and annulled" (563). They were contrary to the nation's history; they were at odds with the nation's Constitution.

As he neared these conclusions in *Worcester*, Marshall indicated that the American nation would inevitably have to come to terms with its heterogeneous makeup. As in other countries, national identity would be built not on the basis of full-scale integration, but on getting used to diversity and acknowledging differences between segments of the population. To be sure, differences among individuals could be softened through legislative measures, but erasing the line of separation between the tribes and the rest of the country was seen as impossible by both the framers and the Court. Indeed, the impracticality of such assimilation was evidenced throughout the world, and not only in the ruins of the French Revolution. For Marshall, "the settled doctrine of the law of nations" offered helpful instruction for the proper relationship between the tribes and the rest of the country (31 U.S. 520). Citing the authority of Swiss legal theorist Emer de Vattel, Marshall noted that a weak state's willingness to place itself under the authority of a stronger state "in order to provide for its safety" did not entail "stripping itself of the right of government, and ceasing to be a state." Even in the present day, Marshall elaborated, "more than one state may be considered as holding its right to self-government under the guarantee and protection of one or more allies." Treating each other as equals in terms of negotiating power and respecting differences between protector and protected nations, such relationships served as analogues for how state and national government alike should approach diplomacy with subnational groups. But it was not Marshall's final model for creating stronger civic bonds.

Constitutional Nationalism

Departing from ethnic and liberal theories, a number of scholars have developed a third theory of nationalism, one based on its social or political construction. The crux of such arguments is neither abstract liberal rights nor homogenous ethnicity, but the forging of national identity through human effort. Perhaps the most prominent spokesperson for this view is the political scientist Benedict Anderson, whose work portrays the modern nation-state as an imagined political community created by the convergence of antiauthoritarian attitudes and the rise of print capitalism.[46] Others argue that nationalism is more closely tied to public policies associated with state building. Thus, while agreeing with Anderson's argument that nationalism is a historically contingent social construct, Ernest Gellner claims that nationalism is tied to the elite manipulation of educational systems and regional labor markets.[47] In recent years, scholars such as Rogers Brubaker and David Laitin have followed along this constructivist path, further underscoring the role of individual agency in creating nationalist sentiment.[48] In such arguments, we find a form of nationalism described in terms not based on fixed ties of kinship, land, or liberal principles. Instead, for these authors nationalism is formed through socialization and mutual recognition, with identity represented as a vibrant and ongoing process rather than a ready-made inheritance.

While these constructivist approaches have enjoyed a great following in Europe, they are also well suited to the United States, where national identity has never stood still long enough to receive fixed definition. As Susan-Mary Grant has put it, nationalism in the United States represents "a process of challenge and debate, reconception and reassessment, a breaking of old traditions and attachments and the forging of new ones."[49] More to our purpose, these constructivist approaches have special resonance when it comes to the influence of the American Constitution in shaping national attachments. Here the idea of "constitutional patriotism" has been influential. Such approaches, articulated perhaps most famously by Jürgen Habermas, suggest a constitution-based identity that in its aspirations is neither universal nor particularistic, but rather is based on the norms, values, and procedures embodied in a liberal democratic constitution.[50] According to Craig Calhoun, this constitutional patriotism is seen as a product of public discourse, in which constitutions are seen not only as legal documents, but also as cultural symbols, providing a site or rallying point to establish a shared sense of community or social solidarity.[51] Although originally directed to actors in the European Union, Habermas's notions have been extended by those such as Jan-Werner Müller to the United States.[52] Indeed, the point is by no means novel, because scholars have long described the American Constitution as a source of social cohesion. As early as 1957, Hans Kohn made the case that the Constitution "represents the life-blood of the American nation, its supreme symbol and manifestation."[53] More recently, Benjamin Barber depicted American political history as an experiment in "grafting the sentiments of patriotism onto a constitutional frame," with the Constitution channeling "the fierce attachments of patriotic sentiment to bond people to high ideals."[54] And in our own time, amid debates over the contingency of culture and the limits of attachment to liberal principles, the Constitution has increasingly come to be seen as a core component of American national identity. As Sanford Levinson has put it, what binds Americans together into a coherent political community is their "constitutional faith."[55] More tangible than liberal rights and yet more ecumenical than ethnic memberships, the Constitution has proven to be a powerful and flexible touchstone of national identity.

In many ways, Marshall's opinions in the Native American cases anticipated the development of a constitutional form of American nationalism. Indeed, the term constitutional nationalism itself was a redundancy for the Chief Justice, because absent the Constitution, there would be no nation. The Marshall Trilogy provided the setting for an elaboration of how American national identity was shaped by the Constitution, a source of national authority and membership for all Americans. As focused as *Johnson* was on comparing the practices of other nations toward the Native American ones, Marshall balances the importance of custom and precedent with "those principles also which our own government has adopted in the particular case and given us as the rule for our decision" (21 U.S. 572). Again in *Cherokee*, the final determination of the legal status of the Cherokee rests on the words of the framers, not alternative sources of legal direction or authority (30 U.S. 18). And in *Worcester*, it was not the Court but the language of the Constitution that had recognized and "sanctioned the previous treaties with the Indian nations, and consequently admits their rank among the powers who are capable of making treaties" (31 U.S. 559). Though the Trilogy frequently invokes historical practices, long-standing traditions, and entrenched attitudes toward the tribes, in the final analysis it was the authority of the Constitution that determined Marshall's judgment of the legality of policies toward the Native American tribes.

Marshall also used the occasion of the Trilogy to remind readers that the Constitution imposed limits on the judiciary itself. It reminds us of a similar admission he made in *Marbury*, but that hardly diminishes how startling it is to hear it from a figure that had now expended years of effort in building up the Court's authority. In *Cherokee*, Marshall admitted that the case had excited the pity of the justices (30 U.S. 15). Yet the Court was restrained from rendering a decision by the clear terms of Article III governing its jurisdiction. Lest this concession be thought a mere pretext to avoid a clash with the political branches, Marshall went a step further. While signaling that a future decision on the validity of Georgia's laws might be given in "a proper case with proper parties," in this instance

Marshall denied that his Court might somehow "control the Legislature of Georgia, and to restrain the exertion of [the statute's] physical force" (30 U.S. 20).[56] Such an interposition, Marshall explained, went far beyond the Court's proper role of "inquiry and decision," amounting to a request that smacked "too much of the exercise of political power to be within the proper province of the judicial department." The practical if not legal work of defending rights, Marshall averred, belonged to tribunals possessing the authority and resources to remedy past wrongs and prevent future ones. Not to be lost in this veiled criticism of the Jackson administration is Marshall's broader message to the tribes: the Court was bound by the positive law of the Constitution, not considerations of natural law, justice, or the simple dictates of human decency.

Beyond the restraints the Constitution imposed on public servants, Marshall's opinions in these cases point to the salutary effects of constitutional government for diminishing violent conflict between Native and non-Native Americans. During the Revolution, the tribes were "restless, warlike, and signally cruel in their irruptions," paying no heed to "the general influence of humanity" (20 U.S. 23). At that time little more than "wandering hordes, held together by ties of blood and habit," the introduction of the rule of law had created an enormous change in Native American life (27). By the 1830s, the tribes had adopted and successfully implemented their own constitutions, juries, and other legal procedures modeled on those of the United States. Thus they now realized that wrongs might find redress at the bar of the Supreme Court of the United States, not on the battlefield. Prior to 1787, Marshall writes in *Worcester*, tribal leaders would have given little thought to "enlightened principles of reason and justice," let alone to the Supreme Court (31 U.S. 590). But times had changed. No longer was this a "fierce and warlike" people in their character, but a political community founded on "the basis of justice and the forms of civilization" (546, 590). To be sure, some of this change was a result of federal measures designed to promote the "humane designs of civilizing the neighbouring Indians," and the distinction between assimilation and preservation in such efforts was blurry (557).[57] But there was no denying that the legal and political differences separating the tribes from the rest of the nation had narrowed. For Marshall, the adoption of American legal practices had increased the attractiveness of judicial solutions to political conflict among the Cherokee. Indeed, at least on this occasion, their respect for the rule of law as expounded by the Court was greater than that of Georgia.

Not to be lost in Marshall's discussion of the change undergone by the Native American tribes was his discussion of the Constitution's security of the civil liberties of all Americans. After all, Samuel Worcester's sentence was the key mechanism for Marshall to finally grant standing and rule on behalf of the tribes. As *Worcester* attested, the constant political danger to individual liberty and minority rights was colorblind. Looming in the background of the case was the state of Georgia's illegal seizure of George "Corn" Tassel, a Cherokee citizen who was subsequently subjected to a show trial and execution that made a mockery of the legal process Marshall had defended for so long.[58] Certainly the rights of internal governance of the Cherokee were endangered by such actions. But, broadly speaking, in *Worcester* Marshall recognized that the rights of all Americans were imperiled by arbitrary state prosecution and punishment. Samuel Worcester and his fellow Christian missionaries confronted the same antagonist as the Native Americans. That the punishment the missionaries faced was less severe did not change its source or mitigate its arbitrariness. As Marshall noted, Worcester and his allies were "seized while performing, under the sanction of the chief magistrate of the Union, those duties which the humane policy adopted by Congress had recommended," and they were subsequently tried and condemned on the basis of acts and procedures that clearly violated the Constitution (31 U.S. 562). Moreover, Worcester was the victim of "disgraceful punishment" by Georgia authorities—"if punishment could disgrace when inflicted on innocence." The implications of Marshall's argument are clear: the case was primarily but not exclusively about Native Americans. If politicians in Georgia were allowed to defy the laws of the nation and its Constitution, it would endanger not only the rights of Native Americans but also the rights of all American citizens. Today it might be only the Native Americans and a few white interlopers whose rights were at risk; tomorrow, Marshall ominously suggests, the state of Georgia might trample underfoot the liberties of all its citizens.

The Marshall Trilogy was not simply about a clash of policies between the states and the federal government, serious as this conflict was. The subtext of the opinions is the struggle concerning the scope and content of nationalism in the United States, conflicting visions destined to come to a head in the coming decades. Marshall emphasized that more was at stake in this fight than the property rights of Native and non-Native Americans. For Marshall, the relationship between the tribes and government authority had changed with the ratification of the Constitution. Like so many other thorny political issues, the Constitution clarified the powers and responsibilities of the central government in relation to the Native nations. Authority to deal with the tribes was no longer divided, as it was between the states and the Continental Congress under the Articles of Confederation. As Marshall put it in *Worcester*, the Constitution endowed Congress with "the powers of war and peace; of making treaties, and of regulating commerce with foreign nations and among the several States and with the Indian tribes" (31 U.S. 559). No longer was the national legislature to serve at the behest of the state governments. On the contrary, all "shackles imposed on this power" were now "discarded," and the national government was vested with full and exclusive power to regulate commerce with the tribes. Thus, Marshall continued, Georgia not only had abandoned a long-standing tradition of noninterference in tribal governance, but also had renounced the Constitution's delegation of authority to Congress. "The whole intercourse between the United States and this nation," intoned Marshall, "is by our constitution and laws vested in the government of The United States" (561). More than acts of Congress and federal treaties, it was the "settled principles of our Constitution" that were being trampled. It was his old foe, states' rights ideology, that he feared might once more upend the nation, and Marshall once again held out the words of the Constitution as a bridle on the state governments.

However, Marshall believed that the Constitution, more than just serving as a bridle, could ameliorate divisions as a distinctly American document. A distant onlooker of the fanaticism and excesses of the French Revolution, he was always skeptical of high philosophy; there are few references in either his private or public papers to the grand principles of the Declaration. As Marshall put it in *Johnson*, consideration of the tribes must be guided by "not singly those principles of abstract justice," regulating "in a great degree, those rights of civilized nations, whose perfect independence is acknowledged" (21 U.S. 572). While a kind of national symbol, the Constitution was a code Americans could actually see and read, a tactile inheritance from the framers and a written testament of national principles. The document avoided the excesses abstract principles not properly conditioned to time and place tend toward, and it was this law that must direct the conduct of the people and the Court alike: the appropriate rules to follow were those set forth by "our own government" in phrases that must be "adopted in the particular case" before the Court as a rule for its decision.[59]

As he had in *Marbury*, *McCulloch*, and *Ogden*, Marshall once again narrated the role that the Constitution exerted over American life. To the casual reader, however, his conduct in the Trilogy may appear contradictory at best and craven at worst: Marshall backed away from defending the ultimate sovereignty of the tribes in *Johnson* and *Cherokee*, then decided to deliver a hollow reprimand to the state of Georgia in *Worcester*. In fact, as in previous opinions, Marshall's pivot point in the Trilogy was the Constitution. In *Cherokee Nation*, the Court was bound by Article III and the commerce clause to restrain indulging its sympathy for the Native American tribes, while in *Worcester* the supremacy clause authorized the Court to nullify Georgia's regulation of the Cherokee. Pointing beyond the admitted importance of ethnic ties and the nation's commitment to liberal principles, it was the Constitution that informed Marshall's nationalism in the Trilogy. A shared regard for its "controlling power" and "settled principles," Marshall suggested forlornly, might very well be the best hope that Native and non-Native Americans might coexist in peace (31 U.S. 536, 561).

Conclusions

Ultimately, Marshall's efforts in the Native American cases did little to change the minds of those he was most concerned with persuading. He could deter neither the combined will of the Congress and President nor the designs of Southern state legislatures. Nor could he halt the expropriation of American Indian lands, which he openly lamented. Yet, for all that, Marshall persevered in his defense of the Constitution and its unifying influence for all Americans.[60] This defense is part of the Trilogy's twist: in light of all the charges of activism leveled at the Marshall Court by its critics, perhaps his most forceful nationalism is stated in one of its greatest defeats. Incapable of making policy, Marshall nonetheless contended that the condition of the Native American tribes required a more delicate and accommodating approach than the one political officers were willing to offer then or (one could argue) since. Even though the days of peaceful coexistence between the tribes and the rest of the country appeared at an end, Marshall would not brook the blatant disregard shown to the Native Americans by state officials, an affront not simply to the Cherokee Nation but also to the historical relationship between tribal and federal governments.

For Americans today, Marshall's words continue to provide food for thought for citizens concerned with the protection of ethnic communities or individuals in a multiracial society. Territorial rights of Native Americans continue to hover over American politics, as indicated by the ongoing controversy over construction of the Dakota Access Pipeline near the Standing Rock Indian Reservation. And Americans still struggle with broader issues related to ethnic diversity, as illustrated by heated debates concerning the regulation of immigration to the United States. While Americans may now hold a more charitable view of ethnic minorities when compared to the 1830s, the tensions between unity and difference continue to pose a fraught dilemma for many Americans, as they did for Marshall. The more things change, the more they stay the same.

Yet at least for Marshall himself, the Trilogy represents his final rallying cry on behalf of a nation dedicated to constitutional government and the rule of law, a commitment he believed was being destroyed by states' rights agitation in the age of Jacksonian democracy. For his part, the Chief Justice was pessimistic about the prospects of constitutional nationalism in his final years on the Court—indeed, about the future of the Constitution itself. In spite of his growing dismay, however, he continued to cling to the document's ability to institute not only a new legal order, but also a form of nationalism that might embrace all inhabitants of the United States.

Only three years after his opinion in *Worcester*, Marshall died in Philadelphia following a brief illness in July 1835. At the time of his passing, the Supreme Court enjoyed power and influence unparalleled prior to his tenure. Indeed, with Marshall as its Chief Justice, the Court had cemented itself as a roughly coequal branch of the national government, with Marshall playing an instrumental if not decisive role in its new standing. But in honoring his legacy, we must go beyond his legal theory to his political philosophy, including the themes of legitimacy, sovereignty, citizenship, and nationalism discussed in this book. Nor are these concepts of merely historical significance. Marshall's words have an abiding topicality across the ages, giving a fresh perspective to our debates about the Constitution today. To the many titles that have been assigned to his name—Federalist, nationalist, the Great Chief Justice—we should add one more: political theorist.

Summation

The Legacy of Marshall's Constitutionalism

Despite his perch at the summit of American legal and constitutional history, John Marshall's political theory has long been shrouded in ambiguity. Marshall is most famous for his constitutional opinions, and his writing was usually restricted to the immediate issues before the Supreme Court. But, like the man himself, his arguments are much more wide-ranging and deliberate—indeed, much more philosophical—than they appear at first glance. Was he a big-government Federalist? A libertarian defender of the free market? A classical republican? In truth, to the extent that any of these labels resonate, they insufficiently capture Marshall's thinking. His constitutionalism contained political dimensions that resist the scholar's attempts to locate Marshall's thought in the conventional categories of legal and historical scholarship. An accurate representation of Marshall as a political thinker must be all-encompassing enough to include his abstract philosophical convictions as well as his practical political assessment of the Constitution's influence on the fledgling United States.

By revisiting some of the most important of Marshall's opinions, we gain better insight into his vision of what values the new nation should impress upon its citizens in its early years. As the nation's fourth Chief Justice, Marshall was in the thick of the difficult task of legitimizing a nation to a people whose identification and sense of citizenship had hitherto stopped at the boundary points of their respective states. Such legitimation was inevitably gradual work and forced Marshall to continually probe the question of what constitutional obligation, sovereignty, and citizenship required. Turning to his opinions reminds us that the national character implied by constitutional government—the Constitution's meaning, scope, and responsibilities—was publicly rethought, discussed, and contested even in the earliest years of the new republic. Amid this dialogue, well into the 1800s it was up to public servants to elevate the Constitution's status in national affairs. Seen in this light, the Marshall Court was not merely engaged in a colloquy with the President, Congress, or state legislatures. His arguments are pitched beyond political officials entirely, to ordinary Americans who, through reading his opinions, might gain a deeper and more detailed understanding of what government under the Constitution entailed. Fully aware that many Americans did not share his particular understanding of constitutional government and the powers of the national government, he never flew into a rage over the fact. In the conversation between citizens and their representatives about the form and substance of the Constitution, he saw a salutary influence for republican self-government.

Naturally, Marshall did not advance his view of the Constitution in a vacuum. He was not the only figure in his time or afterward who claimed the mantle of constitutional interpreter, determined to set the course of the new country.[1] The opinions discussed here give early evidence of the ongoing back-and-forth between the political branches and the Supreme Court concerning constitutional construction that has proven to be rich material for study among political scientists who analyze judicial politics.[2] Over the course of his tenure, Marshall's primary antagonists varied from the Democratic-Republicans to the state governments to President Jackson. In each instance, his attempts to shape public opinion and the actions of political decision makers were beset by these competing factors as well as the formal checks and balances embedded in the Constitution. We must not lose sight of the fact that however self-evident some of Marshall's arguments may appear today, they were often unconvincing and controversial for many of his fellow Americans. He was constrained by outside forces even as he was augmenting the Court's influence.

On some occasions, however, Marshall constrained himself. One such instance was in the case of *Marbury v. Madison*, his most serious engagement with the notion of constitutional legitimacy. More than a case addressing judicial review, *Marbury* involves the Constitution's protection of liberties, its embodiment of popular sovereignty, and its ability to provide legal focal points for the nation as bases for its binding authority. But of even greater significance in *Marbury* is Marshall's theory of the document's moral legitimacy, that is, its institution of a reasonably just legal order that, in the absence of better and realistically attainable alternatives, gave to the nation a system of law superior to other sources of political authority. Never was Marshall's position on the Supreme Court more precarious than at this early juncture, and in few instances was he more vigorous in defense of the Constitution's fundamental binding legitimacy.

Yet legitimacy is only one piece of the puzzle of Marshall's constitutional thought. Years after *Marbury*, he would elaborate on the notion of constitutional sovereignty in the famous case of *McCulloch v. Maryland* and its immediate aftermath. In his opinion, as well as in the acrimonious debate with Judge Spencer Roane that followed the Court's verdict, Marshall described the Constitution's embodiment of both unified and divided sovereignty. But beyond these concepts, he emphasized that the document was itself a source of sovereignty that controlled national and state policies alike. In making this case on behalf of the Constitution as the ultimate political authority in the United States, Marshall temporarily succeeded in quelling fears stoked by Roane and others who saw in *McCulloch* an emasculation of the state governments.

The makeup of the Supreme Court changed with the passage of time. The administrations of Thomas Jefferson and Andrew Jackson and the inevitable turnover in the Court's membership guaranteed that it would no longer be the strong bastion of nationalism that was the calling card of the early Marshall Court. Fissures in the Court became evident in the growing number of divided opinions issued by the Court in the early nineteenth century. Still, Marshall reserved his one dissent on a constitutional question for the case of *Ogden v. Saunders*, a case that addressed a seemingly unremarkable New York bankruptcy statute. Concerned by the implications of the act, which allowed for prospective default provisions to be incorporated into private contracts, he used the occasion to emphasize elements of classical liberalism and republicanism implicit in economic agreements. Moreover, his dissent articulated an understanding of republican liberty based on political nondomination, a type of freedom he believed could only be secured by the Constitution. It was the Court's apparent abandonment of that security to the transient will of political officials that led Marshall to put a crack in the solidarity of the institution that he himself had labored to build up.

Finally, the theme of national identity was addressed in Marshall's trilogy of opinions in the Native American cases: *Johnson v. McIntosh*, *Cherokee Nation v. Georgia*, and *Worcester v. Georgia*. Now staring down hostility from the states as well as the rest of the federal government, in these cases Marshall formulated a theory of national identity that reached beyond ethnic and civic claims to one based on the Constitution.

Although he could do little for the Native American tribes, the theory of constitutional nationalism he points to here sheds light on his belief in the salutary benefits of a broad national identity. More than a mere legal code imposing duties and restrictions on the national government, he portrays the Constitution as a means for national unification. With states' rights sentiment and antipathy toward the Native American tribes reaching a fever pitch, Marshall stood by constitutional principles as a basis for a form of nationalism that could assuage the hostilities he feared might soon tear the nation apart. Ultimately, forces beyond his control dashed his hopes, along with those of the Native Americans. But in our own time, examination of Marshall's political thought in these cases leads to greater recognition of the varieties as well as possible alternatives to contemporary theories of national identity.

What unites the different threads of these arguments is Marshall's commitment to the absolute supremacy of the Constitution and the rule of law. Under its rule, seemingly contradictory notions of popular sovereignty and rights, federalism and nationalism, and liberalism and republicanism are mutually reinforcing for Marshall. While Marshall acknowledged other stakes in such debates, they were less important for him than loyalty to the Constitution. But his constitutional patriotism, such as it was, did not ignore alternative bases of loyalty. Instead, his writing consistently forces readers to reflect on the sufficiency of the political categories raised in a given case, as his arguments in support of the Constitution proceed by way of careful exposition. Thus Marshall's political thought approximates most closely those philosophies that see a role for the Constitution in canalizing and coordinating our differences to establish civic habits on a more peaceful footing than identities tied to either abstractions or inherited traits. Citizenship of this constitutional-patriotic sort, as described by William Booth, stands at the midpoint between "exclusionary, nonpolitical" national memberships and "the nomadic world of itinerants and their neighborhoods."[3]

In his later years on the Court, Marshall's optimism toward a union based on loyalty to the Constitution waned. By the 1830s, tensions between the states and the national government were rapidly reaching a breaking point. Partisanship was at an all-time high. And the unanimity Marshall had worked so hard to achieve as Chief Justice was dissolving before his eyes as Democrat-Republican judges were appointed to the bench. States rights' theories were becoming ever more popular, as was skepticism toward the national government. The nation was headed into uncharted waters,

Marshall believed, and it was not clear the Constitution could continue to steer the American people through these strange new seas—that is, if the people even wished for its guidance. Fluent in the history of ancient Greece and Rome, Marshall was keenly aware of the notion that in the long run all political regimes were ephemeral and subject to the whims of fortune. By the time his tenure on the Court was drawing to a close in 1832, he gloomily predicted to Joseph Story that "the union has been preserved thus far by miracles, and that cannot continue."[4] With the nation on the cusp of the Civil War, one cannot fault his sad prediction of a "constitutional failure."[5] "Powerful and ingenious minds," he warned in *Gibbons v. Ogden*, would try their hardest to convince individuals "through refined and metaphysical reasoning" that the Constitution was "a magnificent structure, indeed, to look at, but totally unfit for use" (22 U.S. 222). He must have believed, in the end, that his adversaries' attempts had succeeded.

Yet the Constitution and the republic endured, thanks in part to other defenders of the Constitution who took Marshall's place. And perhaps, in a time when many have grown weary of the promises and policies of the major political parties, we can now appreciate better than Americans of Marshall's time his political theory. Characterized not merely by a strong central government, Marshall's thought offers up a union whose members were knit together by the letter and spirit of the Constitution. It is a bold vision, and whatever we think of its plausibility, it challenges us at least to reevaluate the received wisdom we may have about Marshall, for he was not simply a legal mind or a propagandist masquerading as a judge. Instead, there was something philosophical and reflective lurking beneath his staid temper, revealed in his abiding concern that his fellow citizens should appreciate the importance of the Constitution and the rule of law for republican self-government. In making such arguments, Marshall's audience extended beyond parties appearing before the Court to encompass all Americans. If he was not a philosopher-statesman on par with figures such as James Madison and Thomas Jefferson, he nevertheless possessed and made known a theory of constitutional government distinct from the dominant schools of thought and rival interpretive camps of his time.

Were he alive today, Marshall would likely find much to dislike about our current politics. Like many of the framers, he would regret the fractured state of American politics today, and deplore the increased politicization of the modern Supreme Court as revealed by heated confirmation battles and polarized divisions among the voting patterns of justices. While he might celebrate the increase of the nation's territory, population, and international standing, he would likely lament the divisions that continue to be drawn among Americans along the lines of geography, politics, class, and race—to name only some of our most salient and enduring forms of discrimination.

Marshall's disappointments, however, would be dwarfed by a sense of wonder that the Constitution remains supreme law of the land, with the Supreme Court as its utmost defender. Of this he would surely be proud. Ever mindful of the fickleness of human nature, however, he would continue to point to the document as an authority for national policy as well as a source of unity—perhaps the only source of unity—at a time of ongoing partisan strife and rancor. His political thought introduces us as readers, as students ourselves of the Constitution, to the fundamental and enduring importance of the rule of law for citizens today. In understanding the bases of Marshall's constitutionalism, we may better articulate our own.

Notes

Introduction

1. The statue is not so imposing that it deters visitors from touching Marshall's toe for good luck (a tradition of unknown origin). I am obliged to Matthew Hofstedt for this anecdote.

2. The best and most concise statement of Marshall's influence on the development of the judiciary remains Max Lerner, "John Marshall and the Campaign of History," *Columbia Law Review* 39, no. 3 (1939): 396–431.

3. John Quincy Adams, "Diary Entry, February 13, 1831," as quoted in Charles Warren, *The Supreme Court in United States History*, vol. II (Boston: Little, Brown and Co. 1922), 212. On Adams's high regard for Marshall, see Michael Daly Hawkins, "John Marshall Through the Eyes of an Admirer: John Quincy Adams," *William & Mary Law Review* 43, no. 4 (2002): 1453–61.

4. Woodrow Wilson, *Constitutional Government in the United States* (New York: Columbia University Press, 1908), 158, 159.

5. Oliver Wendell Holmes, *Collected Legal Papers* (New York: Harcourt, Brace, and Howe, 1920), 270.

6. As Samuel Konefsky notes, "Marshall himself denied that his political philosophy was the product of deliberate reflection or contemplation," instead attributing its emergence to the "casual circumstances" of the American Revolution rather than idle reverie. See his *John Marshall and Alexander Hamilton: Architects of the American Constitution* (New York: Macmillan, 1964), 254.

7. Albert J. Beveridge, *The Life of John Marshall*, 4 vols. (Boston: Houghton Mifflin, 1919).

8. See, for example, Charles F. Hobson, *The Great Chief Justice: John Marshall and the Rule of Law* (Lawrence: University Press of Kansas, 1996), 164–70, 171–74, 177–78; Jean Edward Smith, *John Marshall: Definer of a Nation* (New York: Henry Holt, 1996), 488–89; and R. Kent Newmyer, *John Marshall and the Heroic Age of the Supreme Court* (Baton Rouge: Louisiana State University Press, 2001), 414–58.

9. Harlow Giles Unger, *John Marshall: The Chief Justice Who Saved the Nation* (Philadelphia: De Capo Press, 2014), 321.

10. Lawrence Goldstone, *The Activist: John Marshall, Marbury v. Madison, and the Myth of Judicial Review* (New York: Walker and Company, 2008), 7.

11. Robert H. Bork, *Coercing Virtue: The Worldwide Rule of Judges* (Washington: AEI Press, 2003), 55.

12. William Draper Lewis, *Great American Lawyers* (Philadelphia: John C. Winston Co., 1907), II: 378.

13. Karen Orren and Christopher Walker, for example, have recently shown how Marshall's decision in *Marbury v. Madison* pursued questions related to the Court's jurisdiction while turning aside political concerns implicit in the case. See their "Cold Case File: Indictable Acts and Officer Accountability in *Marbury v. Madison*," *American Political Science Review* 107, no. 2 (2013): 241–58. For other studies of Marshall's use of judicial review in relation to its modern applications, see Leslie Friedman Goldstein, "Popular Sovereignty, the Origins of Judicial Review, and the Revival of Unwritten Law," *Journal of Politics* 48, no. 1 (1986): 51–71; Robert Lawry Clinton, *Marbury v. Madison and Judicial Review* (Lawrence: University Press of Kansas, 1989); and Sylvia Snowiss, *Judicial Review and the Law of the Constitution* (New Haven, CT: Yale University Press, 1990).

14. See the title of Richard Ellis's recent book *Aggressive Nationalism: McCulloch v. Maryland and the Foundation of Federal Authority in the Young Republic* (New York: Oxford University Press, 2007). More evenhanded treatments of Marshall's legal legacy that are nonetheless in accord with its nationalizing effects include Edward S. Corwin, *John Marshall and the Constitution* (New Haven, CT: Yale University Press, 1919); Leonard Baker, *John Marshall: A Life in Law* (New York: Macmillan, 1974); Francis N. Stites, *John Marshall: Defender of the Constitution* (Boston, MA: Little, Brown and Co., 1981); and Mark R. Killenbeck, *McCulloch v. Maryland: Securing a Nation* (Lawrence: University Press of Kansas, 2006).

15. Benjamin N. Cardozo, *The Nature of the Judicial Process* (New Haven, CT: Yale University Press, 1921), 169. On the Supreme Court's inconsequence prior to Marshall's tenure, see James F. Simon, *What Kind of Nation* (New York: Simon and Schuster, 2002), 138–39.

16. See Morton J. Frisch, "John Marshall's Philosophy of Constitutional Republicanism," *Review of Politics* 20, no. 1 (1958): 34–45; and Robert K. Faulkner, *John Marshall's Jurisprudence* (Princeton, NJ: Princeton University Press, 1968), 3–44. For a treatment of Marshall's thought that marries its republican elements to his pragmatist leanings, see Thomas C. Shevory, "John Marshall as Republican: Order and Conflict in American Political History," in *John Marshall's Achievement: Law, Politics, and Constitutional Interpretation*, ed. Thomas C. Shevory (New York: Greenwood Press, 1989), 75–93.

17. Richard A. Brisben, "John Marshall and the Nature of Law in the Early Republic," *The Virginia Magazine of History and Biography* 98, no. 1 (1990): 62.

18. Faulkner (1968) portrays Marshall's understanding of "American Empire" to be of "a peculiar kind," one framed "in means, but not ends" (39). But there were ends. It is true that Marshall at times resists a fixed definition of nationhood, but against Faulkner's viewpoint this book suggests that Marshall's constitutionalism contains positive aspirations for the nation as well as negative restraints on government.

19. See Smith (1996), 497; and Newmyer (2001), 8–9.

20. Bruce Ackerman, *We the People: Foundations* (Cambridge, MA: Harvard University Press, 1991); Bruce Ackerman, *We the People: Transformations* (Cambridge, MA: Harvard University Press, 1998); David A. Strauss, *The Living Constitution* (New York: Oxford University Press, 2010); Ronald Dworkin, *Taking Rights Seriously* (London: Bloomsbury, 2013); and Bruce Ackerman, *We the People: The Civil Rights Revolution* (Cambridge, MA: Harvard University Press, 2014).

21. Jack P. Greene, *Peripheries and Center: Constitutional Development in the Extended Polities of the British Empire and the United States, 1607–1788* (Athens: University of Georgia Press, 1986); Forrest McDonald, *Rights and the Union: Imperium in Imperio, 1776–1876* (Lawrence: University Press of Kansas, 2000); and Alison L. LaCroix, *The Ideological Origins of American Federalism* (Cambridge, MA: Harvard University Press, 2010).

22. Joyce Appleby, "The Social Origins of American Revolutionary Ideology," *The Journal of American History* 64, no. 4 (1978): 935–58; John P. Diggins, *The Lost Soul of American Politics: Virtue, Self-Interest, and the Foundations of Liberalism* (Chicago: University of Chicago Press, 1984); and Michael P. Zuckert, *The Natural Rights Republic: Studies in the Foundation of the American Political Tradition* (Notre Dame, IN: University of Notre Dame Press, 1996).

23. Drew R. McCoy, *The Elusive Republic: Political Economy in Jeffersonian America* (Chapel Hill: University of North Carolina Press, 1980); Bernard Bailyn, *The Ideological Origins of the American Revolution* (Cambridge, MA: Harvard University Press, 1967); and Lance Banning, *The Jeffersonian Persuasion: Evolution of a Party Ideology* (Ithaca, NY: Cornell University Press, 1978).

24. Anthony D. Smith, *National Identity* (Reno: University of Nevada Press, 1991); David Miller, *On Nationality* (New York: Oxford University Press, 1995); and Benedict Anderson, *Imagined Communities* (New York: Verso, 2006).

25. See Habermas's *Between Facts and Norms: Contributions to a Discourse Theory of Democracy*, trans. William Rehg (Cambridge, MA: Polity Press, 1997), 499. See also Jan-Werner Müller, "A European Constitutional Patriotism? The Case Restated," *European Law Journal* 14, no. 5 (2008): 542–57.

26. See Jan-Werner Müller, *Constitutional Patriotism* (Princeton, NJ: Princeton University Press, 2007), 2. Müller suggests that even stable democracies such as the United States may require some sort of "civic minimum" as a "focal point of democratic loyalty" for political institutions to continue to function effectively (5).

27. Pettit has developed his theory over the course of several volumes. See, e.g., his *Republicanism: A Theory of Freedom and Government* (Oxford: Oxford University

Press, 1997); *A Theory of Freedom: The Psychology and Politics of Agency* (Oxford: Oxford University Press, 2001); and *On The People's Terms: A Republican Theory and Model of Democracy* (New York: Cambridge University Press, 2013), 26–74.

28. On the resonance of such poetic constructions and symbols in the United States, see Richard Slotkin, *Gunfighter Nation: The Myth of the Frontier in Twentieth-Century America* (New York: Atheneum, 1992). For similar considerations using a wider lens, consider Eric Voegelin, *The New Science of Politics* (Chicago: University of Chicago Press, 1987).

Chapter 1

1. For recent studies of the long-term consequences of the case, see Paul W. Kahn, *The Reign of Law: Marbury v. Madison and the Construction of America* (New Haven, CT: Yale University Press, 2002); Mark V. Tushnet, ed., *Arguing Marbury v. Madison* (Stanford, CA: Stanford University Press, 2005); Goldstone (2008); and Cliff Sloan and David McKean, *The Great Decision: Jefferson, Adams, Marshall, and the Battle for the Supreme Court* (New York: Public Affairs, 2009). Despite the importance often ascribed to *Marbury*, several scholars have downplayed both the significance of Marshall's opinion and the case's historical relevance to the practice of judicial review in America. See, e.g., Edward S. Corwin, "*Marbury v. Madison* and the Doctrine of Judicial Review," *Michigan Law Review* 12, no. 7 (1914): 538–72; William W. Van Alstyne, "A Critical Guide to *Marbury v. Madison*," *Duke Law Journal* 18, no. 1 (1969): 36–37; David P. Currie, "The Constitution in the Supreme Court: The Powers of the Federal Courts, 1801–1835," *University of Chicago Law Review* 49, no. 4 (1982): 646–724; James M. O'Fallon, "Marbury," *Stanford Law Review* 44, no. 2 (1992): 219–60; Jack N. Rakove, "The Origins of Judicial Review: A Plea for New Contexts," *Stanford Law Review* 49, no. 5 (1997): 1031–64; Michael J. Klarman, "How Great Were the 'Great' Marshall Court Decisions?," *Virginia Law Review* 87, no. 6 (2001): 1113–25; Larry D. Kramer, "The Supreme Court 2000 Term—Foreword: We the Court," *Harvard Law Review* 115 (2001): 4–5; Sanford V. Levinson, "Why I Do Not Teach *Marbury* (Except to Eastern Europeans) and Why You Shouldn't Either," *Wake Forest Law Review* 38 (2002): 553–78; and Mark A. Graber, "Establishing Judicial Review: *Marbury* and the Judicial Act of 1789," *Tulsa Law Review* 38, no. 4 (2003): 609–50. For a good, recent overview of the debate surrounding *Marbury's* proper place in American constitutional history, see Barry Friedman, "The Myths of *Marbury*," in Tushnet (2005), 65–87.

2. See Wilson (1908); Corwin (1919), 66; Cardozo (1921); Alexander M. Bickel, *The Least Dangerous Branch: The Supreme Court at the Bar of Politics* (Indianapolis, IN: Bobbs-Merrill, 1962), 1–33; Konefsky (1964), 87; Faulkner (1968), 200–12; and Stites (1981). Further underscoring Marshall's alleged partisanship is his significant paraphrasing of Alexander Hamilton's reasoning in support of judicial

review in *Federalist #78* to justify the Court's use of the practice in *Marbury*. See Alexander Hamilton, James Madison, and John Jay, *The Federalist*, ed. J. R. Pole (Indianapolis, IN: Hackett, 2005), 411–18.

3. See Akhil Reed Amar, "*Marbury*, Section 13, and the Original Jurisdiction of the Supreme Court," *University of Chicago Law Review* 56, no. 2 (1989): 443–99; Kahn (2002), 118–19; and Robert G. McCloskey, *The American Supreme Court*, 5th ed. (Chicago: University of Chicago Press, 2010), 25–27.

4. See William E. Nelson, "The Eighteenth-Century Background of John Marshall's Constitutional Jurisprudence," *Michigan Law Review* 76 (1978): 893–960; Christopher Wolfe, "John Marshall & Constitutional Law," *Polity* 15, no. 1 (1989): 5–25; Clinton (1989), 79; Hobson (1996); and Newmyer (2001), 162–63.

5. Beveridge (1919, III), 132, 142. For Beveridge, Marshall's deftness was to be celebrated, not criticized: "The assertion [of constitutional supremacy in *Marbury*] . . . was the deed of a great man. One of narrower vision and smaller courage never would have done what Marshall did. In his management and decision of this case, at the time and under the circumstances, Marshall's acts and words were those of a statesman of the first rank" (142–43).

6. On this point, see Lance Banning, "Republican Ideology and the Triumph of the Constitution," *William and Mary Quarterly* 31, no. 2 (1974): 167–88.

7. John Murrin, "A Roof Without Walls: The Dilemma of American National Identity," in *Beyond Confederation: Origins of The Constitution and American National Identity*, ed. Richard Beeman, Stephen Botein, and Edward C. Carter Jr. (Chapel Hill: University of North Carolina Press, 1987), 346.

8. Keith Whittington, *Political Foundations of Judicial Supremacy* (Princeton, NJ: Princeton University Press, 2007), 54.

9. See Thomas Nagel, *Equality and Partiality* (New York: Oxford University Press 1991), 30. For more extensive treatments of the concept of constitutional legitimacy, see Randy E. Barnett, "Constitutional Legitimacy," *Columbia Law Review* 103, no. 1 (2003): 111–48; Frank I. Michelman, "Is the Constitution a Contract for Legitimacy?," *Review of Constitutional Studies* 8, no. 2 (2003): 101–28; Richard H. Fallon Jr., "Legitimacy and the Constitution," *Harvard Law Review* 118, no. 6 (2005): 1787–853; and, perhaps most famously, Carl Schmitt, *Constitutional Theory* (Durham, NC: Duke University Press, 2008), 136–39.

10. Richard H. Fallon Jr., *Implementing the Constitution* (Cambridge, MA: Harvard University Press, 2001), 118. As Rodney Barker remarks, "legitimacy is precisely the belief in the rightfulness of a state, in its authority to issue commands, so that those commands are obeyed not simply out of fear or self-interest, but because they are believed in some sense to have moral authority." See his *Legitimating Identities: The Self-Presentations of Rulers and Subjects* (Cambridge: Cambridge University Press, 2001), 87.

11. As Barnett (2003) puts it, "the problem of constitutional legitimacy is to establish why anyone should obey the command of a constitutionally-valid law" (111).

12. See Habermas (1997), 499; and Müller (2008), 542–57.

13. Fallon (2005), 1790.

14. See Jon Elster, *Ulysses and the Sirens: Studies in Rationality and Irrationality* (Cambridge: Cambridge University Press, 1984); Richard A. Epstein, *Takings: Private Property and the Power of Eminent Domain* (Cambridge, MA: Harvard University Press, 1985); Cass R. Sunstein, "Constitutions and Democracies: An Epilogue," in *Constitutionalism and Democracy*, ed. Jon Elster and Rune Slagstad (New York: Cambridge University Press, 1988), 327–56; Stephen Holmes, *Passions and Constraints* (Chicago: University of Chicago Press, 1995); Adam Przeworski, *Sustainable Democracy* (New York: Cambridge University Press, 1995), 50; Jon Elster, *Ulysses Unbound: Studies in Rationality, Precommitment, and Constraints* (Cambridge: Cambridge University Press, 2000); and Richard A. Epstein, *The Classical Liberal Constitution* (Cambridge, MA: Harvard University Press, 2014).

15. See Edmund S. Morgan, *Inventing the People: The Rise of Popular Sovereignty in England and America* (New York: Norton, 1988), 13–14; Ackerman (1991; 1998); Jason Frank, *Constituent Moments* (Durham, NC: Duke University Press, 2010); and Ackerman (2014).

16. See Larry Alexander and Frederick Schauer, "On Extrajudicial Constitutional Interpretation," *Harvard Law Review* 110, no. 7 (1997), 1359–87; Barry R. Weingast "The Political Foundations of Democracy and the Rule of Law," *American Political Science Review* 91, no. 2 (1997), 245–63; John M. Carey, "Parchment, Equilibria, and Institutions," *Comparative Political Studies* 33, no. 6/7 (2000), 735–61; Larry Alexander and Frederick Schauer, "Defending Judicial Supremacy: A Reply," *Constitutional Commentary* 17, no. 3 (2000), 455–82; and Strauss (2010).

17. To be sure, several arguments concerning legitimacy do not fall neatly within the rights, consent, and settlement silos. The imposition of order on society, the ability of legal rules and institutions to achieve good government in light of social demographics, and the creation of an affective attachment to the nation have all been looked to as sources of constitutional legitimacy. Hence, while the theories discussed in this analysis may represent the most well-known justifications of constitutional authority, they are by no means exhaustive. For a recent overview of some of these alternative theories, see Mark A. Graber, *A New Introduction to American Constitutionalism* (New York: Oxford University Press, 2013), 40–64.

18. For more detailed discussions of the events leading up to the case as well as the arguments presented to the Court, see Alstyne (1969); Smith (1996), 309–26; and Simon (2002), 173–90.

19. Marbury was Adams's nominee for justice of the peace for the District of Columbia.

20. Though Lincoln attended the proceedings, he made no argument on behalf of an irate Thomas Jefferson.

21. See, e.g., Carl J. Friedrich, *Constitutional Government and Democracy* (Boston, MA: Little, Brown and Co., 1941); Owen M. Fiss, "Groups and the Equal

Protection Clause," *Philosophy & Public Affairs* 5, no. 2 (1976): 107–77; Harry N. Hirsch, *A Theory of Liberty: The Constitution and Minorities* (New York: Routledge, 1992); and Friedrich A. Hayek, *The Constitution of Liberty* (Chicago: University of Chicago Press, 2011).

22. See Dworkin, *Taking Rights Seriously* (2013), 165. See also Cass Sunstein's argument that "Constitutions operate as constraints on the governing ability of majorities; they are naturally taken as antidemocratic" and that these protections are encoded in the constitutional text both explicitly (through amendments) and implicitly (through the separation of powers). Quoted in his "Constitutionalism and Democracy: An Epilogue," 327–28.

23. Ronald Dworkin, *Freedom's Law: The Moral Reading of the Constitution* (Cambridge, MA: Harvard University Press, 1996), 21.

24. Ibid., 73.

25. Hamilton et al. (2005), 48.

26. As Corwin (1919) points out, "Marshall, reversing the usual order of procedure, left the question of jurisdiction till the very last, and so created for himself an opportunity to lecture the President on his duty to obey the law and to deliver the commission" (65). For a similar criticism, see Susan Low Bloch and Maeva Marcus, "John Marshall's Selective Use of History in *Marbury v. Madison*," *Wisconsin Law Review* 301, no. 2 (1986): 301–37.

27. John Brigham, "Political Epistemology: John Marshall's Propositions for Modern Constitutional Law," in Shevory (1989), 162.

28. Throughout this book, references to John Marshall's Supreme Court opinions follow the pagination of the official United States Reports.

29. See James W. Ely Jr., "The Marshall Court and Property Rights: A Reappraisal," *John Marshall Law Review* 33, no. 4 (2000): 1023–61: 1048. Robert Faulkner (1968), who is otherwise careful not to exaggerate Marshall's affinity to the natural law tradition, nonetheless argues that Marshall believed property rights were "not much inferior, at least in political importance, to the fundamental right to life itself . . . Marshall considered [the property right] to be unequivocally a natural right" (17).

30. Although it was not the particular case in *Marbury*, the political questions doctrine promulgated therein may be generally viewed as an emancipation of executive powers. It cannot be denied that Marshall limited the scope of judicial authority along with that of the president's: "The province of the court is, solely, to decide on the rights of individuals, not to inquire how the executive, or executive officers, perform duties in which they have a discretion" (5 U.S. 170).

31. Compare John Locke, *Second Treatise of Government*, ed. C. B. Macpherson (Indianapolis, IN: Hackett, 1980), 52–65; and Akhil Reed Amar, "Popular Sovereignty and Constitutional Amendment," in *Responding to Imperfection: The Theory and Practice of Constitutional Amendment*, ed. Sanford V. Levinson (Princeton, NJ: Princeton University Press 1995), 89–116.

32. See Ackerman (2014), 3.

33. Ibid., 6.

34. Ibid., 5. More recently, Ackerman's argument on behalf of consent as the basis of constitutional legitimacy has been taken up by Jack Balkin, who holds that "[p]ast acts create a framework—the written Constitution—that further acts implement." Thus, "popular sovereignty is not only central to the creation of the written framework, it also underwrites the constructions built on top of the framework that flesh it out over time." See his *Living Originalism* (Cambridge, MA: Harvard University Press, 2011), 54.

35. Bruce Ackerman, "The Living Constitution," *Harvard Law Review* 120, no. 7 (2007): 1802.

36. Among its provisions, section 13 authorized issuing "writs of mandamus, in cases warranted by the principles and usages of law, to any courts appointed, or persons holding office, under the authority of the United States" (5 U.S. 173).

37. On the importance of consent for the legitimacy of state constitutions during the Founding period, see Donald S. Lutz, "The Theory of Consent in Early State Constitutions," *Publius* 9, no. 2 (1979): 11–42.

38. Newmyer (2001), 173. Marshall's reasoning bears close resemblance to James Madison's position in *Federalist #45* (2005) that "the public good, the real welfare of the great body of the people is the supreme object to be pursued" by government, and that "as far as the sovereignty of the states cannot be reconciled to the happiness of the people, the voice of every good citizen must be, let the former be sacrificed to the latter" (250, 251). A more radical defense of the Constitution's basis in popular sovereignty was made by James Wilson in his famous speech to the Pennsylvania Ratifying Convention. See *Friends of the Constitution: Writings of the "Other" Federalists, 1787–1788*, ed. Colleen A. Sheehan and Gary L. McDowell (Indianapolis, IN: Liberty Fund, 1998): 71–87.

39. See, for example, Patrick Henry's stirring speech to the Virginia Ratifying Convention in *The Essential Antifederalist*, ed. W. B. Allen and Gordon Lloyd (Lanham, MD: Rowman and Littlefield, 2002): 127–39. On Antifederalist fears of the erosion of state and local government under the proposed Constitution, see Herbert Storing, *What the Anti-Federalists Were for* (Chicago: University of Chicago Press, 1981), 15–23.

40. At least within the context of *Marbury*, it is more of a challenge to determine what Marshall's judgment might be of the importance Ackerman attaches to ongoing public deliberation as an essential reinforcement of the Constitution's legitimacy. On Marshall's general apprehension toward mass democracy, see Faulkner (1968), 147–94. Consider also Leo Strauss, *Natural Right and History* (Chicago: University of Chicago Press, 1965), 102–3.

41. As Larry Alexander and Frederick Schauer (1997) have argued somewhat melodramatically, "an important—perhaps the important—function of law is its ability to settle authoritatively what is to be done" (1377).

42. David A. Strauss, "Common Law, Common Ground, and Jefferson's Principle," *Yale Law Journal* 112, no. 7 (2003): 1733.

43. Strauss (2010), 105.

44. Strauss (2010) has argued that settlement theory is particularly compelling in its ability to justify the Constitution's authority for persons who may have little attachment to the document, the country's traditions, or the founding fathers (104, 102). On this point, see also David A. Strauss, "Legitimacy, 'Constitutional Patriotism,' and the Common Law Constitution," *Harvard Law Review Forum* 126 (2012): 52.

45. John Phillip Reid, *The Concept of Liberty in the Age of the American Revolution* (Chicago: University of Chicago Press, 1988), 68–83.

46. See, for instance, Thomas Jefferson's comment in a letter to Abigail Adams on September 11, 1804: "It is a very dangerous doctrine to consider the judges as the ultimate arbiters of all constitutional questions. It is one which would place us under the despotism of an oligarchy." As quoted in Simon (2002), 189. For a comparison between Marshall's and James Madison's views on constitutional interpretation and authority, see Michael Zuckert, "Epistemology and Hermeneutics in the Constitutional Jurisprudence of John Marshall," in Shevory (1989), 193–216.

47. The authority invested by the Constitution in the judiciary also settled an issue specific to *Marbury*. As Marshall argued, the question of whether a right was vested or not was "in its nature" judicial and so could only be determined by judicial authority (5 U.S. 167).

48. When all eleven thousand words of *Marbury* were published in the nation's newspapers, neither Federalists nor Democratic-Republicans found much to publicly criticize. See Smith (1996), 323–25.

49. Consider Thomas Jefferson's remark to John Dickinson, the chief draftsman of the Articles of Confederation, that the "midnight judges" fiasco showed beyond doubt that the Federalists "have retired into the judiciary as a stronghold, and from that battery all the works of Republicanism are to be beaten down and destroyed" (Simon 2002, 163).

50. Thomas Jefferson, "Letter to Justice Spencer Roane," in *Jefferson: Political Writings*, ed. Joyce Appleby and Terence Ball (New York: Cambridge University Press, 1999), 378, 379.

51. Gordon S. Wood, *Empire of Liberty: A History of the Early Republic, 1789–1815* (New York: Oxford University Press, 2009), 442.

52. Jürgen Habermas, *Communication and the Evolution of Society*, trans. Thomas McCarthy (Boston, MA: Beacon Press, 1979), 178.

53. See William Eskridge and Gary Peller, "The New Public Law Movement: Moderation as a Postmodern Cultural Form," *Michigan Law Review* 89, no. 4 (1991): 747; Joachim J. Savelsberg, "Cultures of Control in Contemporary Societies," *Law and Social Inquiry* 27, no. 3 (2002): 705–6; and John Rawls, *Political Liberalism* (New York: Columbia University Press, 2003), 217.

54. Sotirios A. Barber and James E. Fleming, *Constitutional Interpretation: The Basic Questions* (New York: Oxford University Press, 2007), xii, 65, 160, 165. A more recent exposition is found in James E. Fleming, "Fidelity, Change, and the Good Constitution," *American Journal of Comparative Law* 62, no. 3 (2014): 515–45.

55. Indeed, as A. John Simmons concedes, no existing constitutional regime realizes an absolute moral standard of justice. See his *Justification and Legitimacy* (New York: Cambridge University Press, 2001), 155–56.

56. See David Copp, "The Idea of a Legitimate State," *Philosophy & Public Affairs* 28, no. 1 (1999): 43–44; and Frank I. Michelman, "IDA's Way: Constructing the Respect-Worthy Governmental System," *Fordham Law Review* 72, no. 3 (2003): 358.

57. Fallon (2005), 1798, 1792.

58. Joseph Raz, "On the Authority and Interpretation of Constitutions: Some Preliminaries," in *Constitutionalism: Philosophical Foundations*, ed. Larry Alexander (New York: Cambridge University Press, 2001), 173.

59. See the title of Stites (1981).

60. Randy Barnett also develops an intermediate position between minimalist and maximalist approaches to moral legitimacy, albeit from a perspective more concerned with policy than with constitutions. For Barnett, moral legitimacy is not tied to ideal theories of consent or justice but rather to institutional and procedural qualities affecting the lawmaking process. Hence, a morally legitimate law is one that restricts freedom to the extent necessary to protect others without improperly infringing upon those whose liberties are being restricting. This allows Barnett to offer a theory of legitimacy that makes the concept "a matter of degree rather than an all-or-nothing characteristic." See his *Restoring the Lost Constitution* (Princeton, NJ: Princeton University Press, 2004), 51.

61. On several occasions, Marshall turned to religious language to describe the Constitution and its framers. In *Sturges v. Crowninshield* (1819), Marshall describes the contract clause as embodying a principle the Constitution's framers "intended to hold sacred" (17 U.S. 200). In *United States v. Maurice* (1823), referring to the President's appointment powers, Marshall emphasized he felt "no diminution of reverence for the framers of this sacred instrument, when I say that some ambiguity of expression has found its way into" the appointment clause. And in his dissent in *Ogden v. Saunders* (1827), Marshall described the Court's approach to constitutional questions as one "filled with the sentiments of profound and respectful reverence" (25 U.S. 332). Such remarks reinforce Robert Faulkner's (1968) claim that Marshall endeavored to found a "political religion," one that "dealt not merely with a constitution framed by unusual men, but with a sacred law made by sainted men" (219).

62. See a similar point made by James Madison in *Federalist #49*, who argued that "frequent appeals" to the peoples' judgment "would in great measure deprive the government of that veneration, which time bestows on every thing,

and without which perhaps the wisest and freest governments would not possess the requisite stability." See Hamilton et al. (2005), 274. Marshall's own aversion in *Marbury* to such "frequent appeals" may have something to do with the accrual of veneration described by Madison.

63. Quoted in Smith (1996), 119.

64. In raising these options, one can see Marshall as erecting a positive legal hierarchy that has since been presented in more systematic form by the legal philosopher Hans Kelsen. Kelsen conceives of a state's legal order as a tiered system whose constitutional laws shape and constrain lower, legislative enactments. See, e.g., Hans Kelsen, *An Introduction to the Problems of Legal Theory*, trans. Bonnie Litschewski-Paulson and Stanley L. Paulson (Oxford: Clarendon, 1992), 55–75.

65. Christopher L. Eisgruber, "John Marshall's Judicial Rhetoric," *The Supreme Court Review* (1996): 441.

66. Indeed, perhaps the mere fact of such civic discussion would be a cause for celebration rather than consternation for Marshall if he were alive today.

Chapter 2

1. Christian G. Fritz, *American Sovereigns: The People and America's Constitutional Tradition Before the Civil War* (New York: Cambridge University Press, 2008), 2.

2. Walter Bennett, *American Theories of Federalism* (Tuscaloosa: University of Alabama Press, 1964), 78. Bennett goes on to detail this complexity: sovereignty sometimes "meant powers exercised by governmental organs and sometimes what was represented as the source of these powers. Occasionally it referred to indivisible power and at other times to power which was assumed to be capable of division" (78).

3. Stephen M. Griffin, *American Constitutionalism: From Theory to Politics* (Princeton, NJ: Princeton University Press, 1996), 23.

4. Hugh Willis, "The Doctrine of Sovereignty under the United States Constitution," *Virginia Law Review* 15, no. 4 (1929): 437.

5. Consider Corwin (1919), 130–31; Baker (1974), 594–95; Stites (1981), 130; Killenbeck (2006), 7–8; and Whittington (2007), 111.

6. See Clinton (1989), 192–98; and Smith (1996), 445. G. Edward White sees *McCulloch* as emphasizing both national and state identities in his celebrated work *The Marshall Court and Cultural Change* (New York: Oxford University Press, 1991), 563. In a similar vein, Hobson (1996) contends that Marshall's nationalism is often exaggerated, citing Marshall's attempt in *McCulloch* to balance state, federal, and local political authority (122–24, 247). Finally, consider Judge Clarence Thomas's dissenting opinion in *U.S. Term Limits v. Thornton* (1995), where special emphasis is given to *McCulloch*'s defense of the reserved powers of the state governments. As discussed in Martin S. Flaherty, "John Marshall, *McCulloch v. Maryland*, and

'We the People': Revisions in Need of Revising," *William and Mary Law Review* 43, no. 4 (2002): 1359–67.

7. Sotirios A. Barber, *The Fallacies of States' Rights* (Cambridge, MA: Harvard University Press, 2013), 6, 8. Others have argued that *McCulloch*'s aims were primarily economic rather than political. See Harold J. Plous and Gordon E. Baker, "*McCulloch v. Maryland*: Right Principle, Wrong Case," *Stanford Law Review* 9, no. 4 (1957): 730; Faulkner (1968), 80–81; and Ira L. Strauber, "*McCulloch* and 'The Dilemmas of Liberal Constitutionalism," in Shevory (1989), 137–58. With respect to the shadow the nation's economic affairs cast over the case, see Joseph M. Lynch, "*McCulloch v. Maryland*: A Matter of Money Supply," *Seton Hall Law Review* 18, no. 2 (1988): 223–329.

8. Gerald Gunther, "Introduction," in *John Marshall's Defense of McCulloch v. Maryland* (Stanford, CA: Stanford University Press, 1989), 18, 19. While Gunther presents the *Gazette* articles as evidence against nationalist readings of *McCulloch*, he does not draw direct attention to Marshall's discussion of constitutional sovereignty in these articles.

9. The following reconstruction of *McCulloch* is culled from extensive narratives of the case found in Stites (1981), 129–36; Smith (1996), 440–45; and Simon (2002), 271–78. Good article-length overviews of *McCulloch* are provided in David S. Bogen, "The Scandal of Smith and Buchanan: The Skeletons in the *McCulloch v. Maryland* Closet," *Maryland Law Forum* 9, no. 4 (1985): 125–32; A. I. L. Campbell, " 'It Is a *Constitution* We Are Expounding': Chief Justice Marshall and the 'Necessary and Proper' Clause," *Journal of Legal History* 12, no. 3 (1991), 190–245; and Daniel A. Farber, "The Story of *McCulloch*: Banking on National Power," in *Constitutional Law Stories*, ed. Michael C. Dorf (New York: Foundation Press, 2004), 34–67. Surprisingly, Gunther (1989) and Killenbeck (2006) are the only book-length scholarly treatments of this famous decision.

10. A congressional investigation in early 1819 revealed widespread malfeasance among the Bank's eighteen branches that led to the resignation of the Bank's first president, William Jones. However, a subsequent effort to revoke the Bank's charter failed just as closing arguments in *McCulloch* took place. See Gunther (1989), 3–4; and Simon (2002), 272.

11. For some, the rapidity of the Court's decision suggests that the outcome of *McCulloch* was a foregone conclusion and that Marshall's opinion was composed long before arguments concluded. See, e.g., Lee Epstein and Thomas G. Walker, *Constitutional Law for a Changing America* (Los Angeles: CQ Press, 2015), 111. Beveridge (1919) admits that as *McCulloch* is one of Marshall's longest and "most carefully prepared" opinions, "it seems not unlikely that much of it had been written before the argument" in light of the Court's busy schedule in 1819 (IV, 290). Gunther (1989), however, concludes that the swift release of Marshall's *Gazette* essays "corroborates the conclusion that *McCulloch* was indeed written in response to the week-and-a-half-long argument, not in advance" (18). Moreover, as Lackland

Bloom points out in his recent *Do Great Cases Make Bad Law?* (New York: Oxford University Press, 2014), the question concerning the constitutionality of the Bank had previously been explored in the early days of the Washington administration, and Marshall's opinion was able to lean heavily on the able arguments of Pikney and Webster. Thus, Bloom concludes, "despite the deceptively short time frame in which the opinion was written, Marshall had all the time that he needed" (38).

12. As Marshall summarized the matter, "the powers given to the government imply the ordinary means of execution," and the Bank's incorporation was hardly an extraordinary measure for achieving a constitutionally valid end (17 U.S. 409). At least one scholar otherwise sympathetic to Marshall suggests that his reasoning is unconvincing on this point: "A national bank was undoubtedly a *convenient* and *logical* means, but it was hardly an 'ordinary' means." See David S. Schwartz, "Misreading *McCulloch v. Maryland*," *Journal of Constitutional Law* 18, no. 1 (2015): 58.

13. To this day, little information is available about the Richmond Junto's clandestine membership and operation. As Ellis (2007) describes, "Although there is a large body of literature on the Richmond Junto, there is no consensus among scholars about who its members were, how coherent it was, how it operated, how influential and powerful it was, its overall significance, and even whether it existed at all" (235–36).

14. Daniel Walker Howe notes that even the Republican Party had come around to endorse the Second Bank by 1816 in his *What Hath God Wrought: The Transformation of America, 1815–1848* (New York: Oxford University Press, 2007), 145. On the general political consensus regarding the Bank's validity, see also Klarman (2001), 1128–29.

15. As Bennett (1964) describes, even the draconian Stamp Act of 1765 was defended by supporters of Parliament in America and England "by invoking the conception of absolute and indivisible sovereignty commonly attributed to the sixteenth-century Frenchman Jean Bodin" (21).

16. Gordon S. Wood, *The Creation of the American Republic, 1776–1787* (Chapel Hill: University of North Carolina Press, 1969), 350. Students of law were particularly familiar with the unitary character of sovereignty from their reading of Sir William Blackstone, whose *Commentaries on the Laws of England* enjoyed widespread popularity upon the publication of the first American edition in 1803. See Wilfrid Prest, *William Blackstone: Law and Letters in the Eighteenth Century* (New York: Oxford University Press, 2008), 292. As Gary McDowell describes in his *Language of Law and the Foundations of American Constitutionalism* (New York: Cambridge University Press, 2010), "Blackstone's commitment to absolute sovereignty was firm. The safety and happiness of the individual citizens depended upon it. Without a supreme sovereign with unrestrained compulsive power to enforce the law, the absolute rights of the people would enjoy no security" (211).

17. McDonald (2000), 2.

18. Marshall's interpretation of the necessary and proper clause borrowed significantly from the reasoning of another Federalist stalwart, Alexander Hamilton. In *Federalist #33*, Hamilton had declared that with respect to the question of who was the proper judge "of the necessity and propriety of the laws" of the nation, "the National Government, like every other, must judge in the first instance, of the proper exercise of its powers, and its constituents in the last." Like Marshall, Hamilton also rejected a narrow reading of "necessary" and favored a more expansive rendering as implying "convenient." See Hamilton et al. (2005), 124–25. Marshall would later applaud Hamilton's defense of the Bank as "a copious and perspicuous argument" in the first edition of his *Life of George Washington*, 5 vols. (Philadelphia: C.P. Wayne, 1804–7), V: 294.

19. For recent critiques of the notion of unitary sovereignty, consider Hent Kalmo and Quentin Skinner, eds., *Sovereignty in Fragments: The Past, Present and Future of a Contested Concept* (New York: Cambridge University Press, 2010), ff.

20. LaCroix (2010), 107.

21. Bailyn (1967), 198.

22. Hamilton et al. (2005), 210.

23. On the attitude of the founding generation toward theories of political sovereignty in general, see Adam Tate, "James Madison and State Sovereignty, 1780–1781," *American Political Thought* 2, no. 2 (2013): 176–77. Wood (1969) points out that "the problem of sovereignty was not solved by the Declaration of Independence. It continued to be the most important theoretical question of political throughout the following decade, the ultimate abstract principle to which nearly all arguments were sooner or later reduced" (354).

24. Ira L. Strauber, *Neglected Policies: Constitutional Law and Legal Commentary as Civic Education* (Durham, NC: Duke University Press, 2002), 109.

25. A tension should be mentioned here between Marshall's defenses of national supremacy and coordinate powers. A critic might argue that he is trying to have things both ways; a supporter might respond that he is capable of seeing shades of nuance in government power that his opponents cannot or will not recognize.

26. For example, Marshall's discussion of the Tenth Amendment in *McCulloch* is often cited as evidence of Marshall's nationalism. There he emphasizes the amendment's omission of the word "expressly" from the powers delegated to the national government as confirmation of the framers' intentions to grant a broad range of legal authority to the national government (17 U.S. 406). But even in this instance, Marshall gestures beyond national and state power to the mediating role of the Constitution, declaring that "whether the particular power which may become the subject of contest has been delegated to the one Government . . . or prohibited to the other" depends ultimately "on a fair construction of the whole instrument."

27. As Newmyer (2001) recounts, Marshall's early "Friend to the Union" essays were badly mishandled during the printing process and at Marshall's urging were reprinted with substantial corrections in the *Gazette*. For this reason,

the nine *Gazette* essays should be viewed as Marshall's authoritative defense of *McCulloch* (884).

28. The debate between Marshall and Roane is also analyzed in William E. Dodd, "Chief Justice Marshall and Virginia, 1813–1821," *American Historical Review* 12, no. 4 (1907): 776–87; Charles G. Haines, *The Role of the Supreme Court in American Government and Politics, 1789–1835* (New York: Russell & Russell, 1960), 357–68; Samuel R. Olken, "John Marshall and Spencer Roane: An Historical Analysis of the Conflict over U.S. Supreme Court Appellate Jurisdiction," *Journal of Supreme Court History* 14 (1990), 125–41; White (1991), 552–67; and Ellis (2007), 111–42.

29. Gunther (1989), 52.

30. Beveridge (1919) points out that as president of the Court of Appeals of Virginia, Roane possessed a legal acumen more than capable of confronting Marshall's logic in *McCulloch*. Indeed, he was widely seen as President Jefferson's preferred choice as Marshall's replacement as chief justice of the Supreme Court (III, 114–15).

31. As quoted in Smith (1996), 448.

32. As Kent Newmyer puts it, although Marshall could only dimly perceive the particular historical course on which states' rights theory might lead the nation, experience had taught him "to read history in a tragic light," and the Chief Justice was greatly concerned in *McCulloch*'s immediate aftermath "that the rousing oratory of Virginia radicals would convert the Constitution into the old Confederation." See his "John Marshall, *McCulloch v. Maryland*, and the Southern States' Rights Tradition," *John Marshall Law Review* 33, no. 4 (2000): 883.

33. Parenthetical citations of Marshall's "Friend of the Constitution" essays, Spencer Roane's "Hampden" articles, and William Brockenbrough's "Amphictyon" pieces refer to their collection in Gunther (1989).

34. Lest the Court's critics forget, the point is underlined by "A Friend," who cites this passage in *McCulloch* as proof that "in no single instance does the court admit the unlimited power of congress to adopt any means whatever, and thus to pass the limits prescribed by the constitution" (186–87).

35. Hampden described a consolidated government as one that acted solely upon individuals, bypassing both states and their governments. Marshall acknowledged that the laws of the national government did act upon individuals, but maintained that Hampden had largely ignored the authority retained by state governments under the Constitution ("Friend," 193–94).

36. Once again, the nation's experience with the Articles was instructive: "Under the confederation," Marshall reminded his readers, "congress could do scarcely any thing, [so long as] that body could only make requisitions on the states" ("Friend," 163).

37. In light of Marshall's defense of the Constitution's settlement function in *Marbury*, the document's protection of federalism may be seen as one more example of the many focal points he saw scattered through the constitutional text.

The powers of the general government stipulated in Articles I and V show the way to determining the legality of actions by the states and general government, just as presidential powers set out in Article II provide the key to ascertaining the validity of William Marbury's commission.

38. Populist opposition to the Bank was not easily squelched. When President Andrew Jackson vetoed the renewal of the Second Bank's charter in 1832, he described the Bank in positively demonic terms: "The Bank of the United States . . . was a monster, a hydra-headed monster, . . . equipped with horns, hoofs, and tail and so dangerous that it impaired the morals of our people, corrupted our statesmen, and threatened our liberty." Quoted in Robert V. Remini, *Andrew Jackson and the Bank War* (New York: Norton, 1967), 1.

Chapter 3

1. Stites (1981), 111.
2. Vernon Louis Parrington, *Main Currents in American Thought: The Romantic Revolution in America, 1800–1860* (New York: Harcourt, Brace and Co., 1927), 23.
3. Lerner (1939), 401, 420.
4. Faulkner (1968), 28, 30.
5. Konefsky (1964), 137.
6. Richard K. Matthews, "*Marshall v. Jefferson*: Beyond 'Sanctimonious Reverence' for a 'Sacred' Law," in Shevory (1989), 120. In his *People's History of the Supreme Court* (New York: Viking, 1999), Peter Irons argues that Marshall's commitment to economic liberty crowded out whatever importance he ascribed to other individual rights (141).
7. Walter Berns, "The Supreme Court as Republican Schoolmaster: Constitutional Interpretation and the 'Genius of the People,'" in *The Supreme Court and American Constitutionalism*, ed. Bradford P. Wilson and Ken Masugi (Lanham, MD: Rowman & Littlefield, 1998), 3–16.
8. Newmyer (2001), 261. On Newmyer's account, contract was the crucial link between economic liberalism and classical republicanism for Marshall: "Not only did contract law liberate individual economic energy, it harnessed that energy to the collective prosperity and well-being of society . . . For Marshall, possessive individualism and republican community were inseparable." Indeed, "like other American conservatives of his age, Marshall had no complaint against rapid, even transformative, change as long as it could be controlled" (265). Newmyer even goes so far as to conclude that *Ogden* illustrates Marshall's commitment to making the Court "the ultimate guardian of republican values in a liberal age" and was crestfallen that his fellow justices abandoned the cause (266).
9. See his excellent "John Marshall as Republican" in Shevory (1989), 90.
10. White (1988), 9, 74.

11. Bruce Ackerman, "Constitutional Politics/Constitutional Law," *Yale Law Review* 99, no. 3 (1989): 491.

12. See Ely Jr. (2000), 1028, 1029. As Ely puts it, "The framers of the Constitution and Bill of Rights wove guarantees of private property into the constitutional fabric of the new nation. Marshall and his colleagues, however, were instrumental in giving vitality to the property-conscious values of the framers. In so doing, they did much to set the parameters of American constitutionalism for more than a century" (1060). But unlike (e.g.) James Madison, Ely sees the Marshall Court's defense of property rights "as a means to bring about economic growth, not as a shield merely to safeguard existing interests" (1058).

13. See Stephen A. Siegel, "Rebalancing Professor Ely's Reappraisal of the Marshall Court and Property Rights," *John Marshall Law Review* 33, no. 4 (2000): 1172. On the ambiguous definition of property in the early years of the American republic, Siegel notes that many citizens "extolled property rights but were divided over rights of privilege. Wealth in nineteenth-century America was not a unitary concept" (1170).

14. Consider, for example, the famous Depression-era case of *Home Building & Loan Association v. Blaisdell* (1934), in which the state of Minnesota's suspension of creditors' remedies was declared not to be a violation of the contract clause in light of exigent economic conditions. In his majority opinion, Chief Justice Charles Hughes cited passages from both Marshall's dissent in *Ogden* (the great "mischief" of state legislatures that "interfered with contracts") in addition to his majority opinion in *McCulloch* ("We must never forget that it is a constitution we are expounding"). In doing so, Hughes indirectly points to the interplay between Marshall's liberalism and republicanism present in Marshall's dissent (290 U.S. 428, 443).

15. Christopher Eisgruber (1996) is an important exception, seeing Marshall's invocation of state of nature theory and the framers' private opinions as "a remarkable departure" from his other Supreme Court opinions (470).

16. In *Sturges*, Marshall allowed "that until the power to pass uniform laws on the subject of bankruptcies be exercised by Congress, the states are not forbidden to pass a bankrupt law provided it contain no principle" violating the contract clause (17 U.S. 196–97).

17. As quoted in Jonathan B. Baker, "Has The Contract Clause Counter-Revolution Halted? Rhetoric, Rights, and Markets in Constitutional Analysis," *Hastings Constitutional Law Quarterly* 12, no. 1 (1984): 79.

18. Marshall was joined in his dissent by Associate Justices Gabriel Duvall and Joseph Story.

19. Louis Hartz, *The Liberal Tradition in America* (New York: Harvest, 1991), 11. For a recent reappraisal and defense of the Hartzian thesis, see John W. Kingdon, *America the Unusual* (Belmont, CA: Wadsworth, 1999). Consider also the work of one of Hartz's foremost contemporaries, Richard Hofstadter, who reaches a similar verdict concerning liberalism's influence in the United States in his *The American Political Tradition and the Men Who Made It* (New York: Vintage, 1989), 3–22.

20. Diggins (1984), 14.

21. Zuckert (1996), 4.

22. In his recent biography of Marshall, John Richard Paul holds that that Marshall had "already shaped the contour of American capitalism" notwithstanding his defeat in *Ogden* and that "the conditions for free enterprise to flourish in the nineteenth century" had been a direct result of the Court's decisions. See his *Without Precedent: Chief Justice John Marshall and His Times* (New York: Penguin, 2018), 383.

23. As Newmyer (2001) suggests, "the fundamental error in the majority's position was to assume 'that it is not the stipulation an individual makes which binds him [to contractual performance], but some declaration of the supreme power of a state to which he belongs'" (262).

24. In *Cohens v. Virginia* (1821), Marshall made a similar argument regarding the unifying role of commerce: "That the United States form, for many and for most important purposes, a single nation has not yet been denied. In war, we are one people. In making peace, we are one people. *In all commercial regulations, we are one and the same people.* In many other respects, the American people are one . . ." (19 U.S. 413–14; emphasis added).

25. See Clinton Rossiter, *Seedtime of the Republic* (New York: Harcourt, Brace and Co., 1953); Neal Riemer, "The Republicanism of James Madison," *Political Science Quarterly* 69, no. 1 (1954): 45–64; Douglas Adair, " 'That Politics May Be Reduced to a Science': David Hume, James Madison, and the Tenth *Federalist*," *Huntington Library Quarterly* 20, no. 4 (1957): 343–60; and Caroline Robbins, *The Eighteenth-Century Commonwealthman: Studies in the Transmission, Development, and Circumstance of English Liberal Thought from the Restoration of Charles II until the War with the Thirteen Colonies* (Cambridge, MA: Harvard University Press, 1967).

26. See Perry Miller, "From the Covenant to the Revival," in *Religion in American Life: The Shaping of American Religion*, ed. James Ward Smith and A. Leland Jamison, vol. I (Princeton, NJ: Princeton University Press, 1961), 322–68; Cecelia M. Kenyon, "Republicanism and Radicalism in the American Revolution: An Old-Fashioned Interpretation," *William and Mary Quarterly* 19, no. 2 (1962): 153–82; and Richard Buel Jr., "Democracy and the American Revolution: A Frame of Reference," *William and Mary Quarterly* 21, no. 2 (1964): 165–90.

27. Bailyn (1967), 38–39.

28. Wood (1969) argued that Americans were engaged in "nothing less than a reordering of eighteenth-century society and politics as they had known and despised them—a reordering that was summed up by the conception of republicanism" (47–48). Unlike other authors such as Lance Banning, Wood believed that antifederalist thought marked the end point of classical republican ideas in America. Still, he had no qualms about once stating that "in 1787, classical republicanism was the basic premise of American thinking—the central presupposition behind all other ideas." See his "Intellectual Origins of the American Constitution," *National Forum* 64, no. 4 (1984): 7.

29. See J. G. A. Pocock, *The Machiavellian Moment: Florentine Political Thought and the Atlantic Republican Tradition* (Princeton, NJ: Princeton University Press, 1975), esp. 3, 156–218, 383–400, and 526–27. Pocock's criticism of the "myth" of Locke's influence in America is found at 545. A more succinct statement of Pocock's project is found in his "Virtues, Rights, and Manners: A Model for Historians of Political Thought," *Political Theory* 9, no. 3 (1981): 353–68.

30. Robert Shalhope noted that despite the efforts of Bailyn, Wood, Pocock, and others, republicanism in eighteenth-century America lacked any unified definition beyond "an absence of aristocracy and monarchy," while Paul Rahe has claimed that North America inherited a thoroughly modern tradition whose realism was entirely at odds with classical and medieval political thought. See Shalhope's "Toward a Republican Synthesis: The Emergence of an Understanding of Republicanism in American Historiography," *William and Mary Quarterly* 29, no. 1 (1972): 49–80, 72, and Rahe's *Republics Ancient and Modern: Classical Republicanism and the American Revolution* (Chapel Hill: University of North Carolina Press, 1992). Others who are skeptical of the continuity between colonial America and the classical world include Joyce Appleby, "Republicanism and Ideology," *American Quarterly* 37, no. 4 (1985): 463–71; Steven M. Dworetz, *The Unvarnished Doctrine: Locke, Liberalism, and the American Revolution* (Durham, NC: Duke University Press, 1990); and Daniel T. Rodgers, "Republicanism: The Career of a Concept," *Journal of American History* 79, no. 1 (1992): 37–38. Finally, Richard K. Matthews's books on Thomas Jefferson and James Madison play up the radically new character of American politics in the republic's formative years. See his *Radical Politics of Thomas Jefferson: A Revisionist View* (Lawrence: University Press of Kansas, 1984) and *If Men Were Angels: James Madison and the Heartless Empire of Reason* (Lawrence: University Press of Kansas, 1995).

31. Banning (1978), 13–18. Some authors have argued that classical republican influences extended even into the nineteenth century. See, e.g., Rowland Berthoff, "Independence and Attachment, Virtue and Interest: From Republican Citizen to Free Enterpriser, 1787–1837," in *Uprooted Americans*, ed. Richard L. Bushman, Neil Harris, David Rothman, Barbara Miller Solomon, and Stephen Thernstrom (Boston, MA: Little, Brown and Co., 1979), 99–124; and John Murrin, "The Great Inversion, or Court versus Country: A Comparison of the Revolution Settlements in England (1688–1721), and America (1776–1816)," in *Three British Revolutions: 1641, 1688, 1776*, ed. J. G. A. Pocock (Princeton, NJ: Princeton University Press, 1980), 368–453. For a recent overview of the large readership the classics enjoyed in late eighteenth-century America, see Caroline Winterer, *The Culture of Classicism: Ancient Greece and Rome in American Intellectual Life, 1780–1910* (Baltimore, MD: Johns Hopkins University Press, 2002).

32. McDowell (2010) speculates that such theorists surely included those with whom Marshall and the framers had an "easy familiarity," notably "Grotius, Hobbes, Pufendorf, Locke, Vattel, Burlamaqui, Rutherforth, Blackstone, and Montesquieu" (314).

33. John G. Gunnell, *Imagining the American Polity: Political Science and the Discourse of Democracy* (University Park: Penn State University Press, 2004), 30.

34. John Murrin, "Self-Interest Conquers Patriotism: Republicans, Liberals, and Indians Reshape the Nation," in *The American Revolution: Its Character and Limits*, ed. Jack P. Greene (New York: New York University Press, 1987), 224–29.

35. For this point, see Joyce Appleby, *Capitalism and a New Social Order: The Republican Vision of the 1790s* (New York: New York University Press, 1984), 18.

36. See John T. Agresto, "Liberty, Virtue, and Republicanism: 1776–1787," *Review of Politics* 39, no. 4 (1977): 473–504; Ralph Lerner, *The Thinking Revolutionary: Principle and Practice in the New Republic* (Ithaca, NY: Cornell University Press, 1987), 195–221; and Jean Yarbrough, "The Constitution and Character: The Missing Critical Principle?," in *To Form a More Perfect Union: The Critical Ideas of the Constitution*, ed. Herman Belz, Ronald Hoffman, and Peter J. Albert (Charlottesville, VA: University of Virginia Press, 1992), 217–49.

37. As described in Ralph Lerner, "Commerce and Character: The Anglo-American as New-Model Man," *William and Mary Quarterly* 36, no. 1 (1979): 3. As Lerner puts it, such thinkers identified a "complex, ever-changing interdependence" arising from commercial exchange, an interdependence indirectly facilitated by all those who "labored intently to satisfy" personal wants. In doing so, "men would become commercial cousins, cool fellow-citizens of a universal republic" (11). See also Stephen Miller, "Adam Smith and the Commercial Republic," *Public Interest* 61 (1980): 106–22.

38. Thomas L. Pangle, *The Spirit of Modern Republicanism: The Moral Vision of the American Founders and the Philosophy of Locke* (Chicago: University of Chicago Press, 1988), 126.

39. Prominent explanations of this principle include Pocock (1981), 186–212; Quentin Skinner, *Liberty Before Liberalism* (New York: Cambridge University Press, 1998); Pettit (1997, 2001); Quentin Skinner, "The Idea of Negative Liberty: Machiavellian and Modern Perspectives," *Visions of Politics* II (Cambridge: Cambridge University Press, 2002), 186–212; Maurizio Viroli, *Republicanism*, trans. Antony Shugaar (New York: Hill and Wang, 2002); John W. Maynor, *Republicanism in the Modern World* (Cambridge: Polity Press, 2003); Quentin Skinner, "Freedom as the Absence of Arbitrary Power," in *Republicanism and Political Theory*, ed. Cécile Laborde and John Maynor (Malden, MA: Blackwell, 2008), 83–101; and Victoria M. Costa, "Neo-Republicanism, Freedom as Non-Domination, and Citizen Virtue," *Politics, Philosophy & Economics* 8, no. 4 (2009): 401–19.

40. Skinner (1998), 11fn31, 54–55fn174, 176.

41. The principal foil for Skinner and Pettit is Sir Isaiah Berlin, whom Skinner has criticized for assuming "that negative liberty is jeopardized only be coercive interference" (115). In fact, Skinner argues, "it will always be necessary for the state to ensure . . . that its citizens do not fall into a condition of avoidable dependence on the goodwill of others." (119). For Berlin's argument, see Isaiah

Berlin, "Two Concepts of Liberty," in *Four Essays on Liberty* (Oxford: Oxford University Press, 1992), 118–72.

42. Pettit (1997) suggests that freedom is compromised even in those circumstances where arbitrary coercion is merely a danger rather than a certainty. In a particularly vivid example, he describes the misery of slavery as issuing as much from the constant prospect of lashings as the punishment itself (99, 55).

43. Neo-republicans such as Pettit are not opposed to political interference as such. Rather, the key desideratum of their theories is the avoidance of arbitrary interference. In isolation, neither negative liberty (emphasizing noninterference) nor positive liberty (emphasizing self-determination) can secure this goal. Rather, nonarbitrary interference, which Pettit (1997) roughly defines as public interests shared by all citizens, is best achieved via the institutions and checks supplied by a neo-republican political and legal framework (55).

44. See Pettit (1997), 21. Pettit claims his neo-republicanism echoes seventeenth-century notions of "people's rights under the law," especially "rights against the powerful" (22–23). Furthermore, Pettit claims that this idea of nondomination finds expression in the agonistic, "contestatory" citizenship familiar to the earlier republican thought of Polybius, Cicero, and Livy. On this point, see Philip Pettit, "Two Republican Traditions," in *Republican Democracy: Liberty, Law, and Politics*, ed. Andreas Niederberger and Philipp Schink (Edinburgh: Edinburgh University Press, 2013), 171.

45. Philip Pettit, *Just Freedom* (New York: Norton, 2014), 4. As Pettit (1997) describes the idea elsewhere, "enslavement and subjection are the great ills, and independence and status the supreme goods" (132).

46. On the differences between this version of republicanism and that of the Atlantic tradition, consider Quentin Skinner, *The Foundations of Modern Political Thought*, 1 (Cambridge: Cambridge University Press, 1978), 69–112; and Skinner, "The Republican Ideal of Political Liberty," in *Machiavelli and Republicanism*, ed. Gisela Bock, Quentin Skinner, and Maurizio Viroli (New York: Cambridge University Press, 1990), 293–309. A number of scholars have argued that the differences separating liberalism from republicanism are ones of degree rather than kind. For instance, see Richard Dagger, "Autonomy, Domination, and the Republican Challenge to Liberalism," in *Autonomy and the Challenges to Liberalism: New Essays*, ed. John Christman and Joel Anderson (Cambridge: Cambridge University Press, 2005), 177–203; and Efraim Podoksik, "One Concept of Liberty: Toward Writing the History of a Political Concept," *Journal of the History of Ideas* 71, no. 2 (2010): 232–33. Andreas Kalyvas and Ira Katznelson go so far as to argue that republicanism gave birth to liberal theory, claiming that "liberalism as we know it was born from the spirit of republicanism, from attempts to adapt republicanism to the political, economic, and social revolutions of the eighteenth century and the first decades of the nineteenth." See their *Liberal Beginnings: Making a Republic for the Moderns* (New York: Cambridge University Press, 2008), 4.

47. Newmyer (2001) argues that the argument made by several historians that classical liberalism and republicanism are "not at odds . . . is especially applicable to Marshall" (494).

48. As Pettit (2002) notes in differentiating neo-republicanism from Berlin's concept of negative liberty, "to enjoy non-domination . . . is to be possessed, not just of non-interference by arbitrary powers, but of a secure or resilient variety of such non-interference" (69).

49. In his discussion of the pre-political origins of contract, Marshall distinguishes natural coercion from political coercion. Because it would be "incompatible with general peace," he notes, society "prohibits the use of private individual coercion" and places redress on a "more safe and more certain" legal basis (25 U.S. 350).

50. Beveridge (1919) writes that Marshall "feared that sheer majorities would be unjust, intolerant, tyrannical; and he was certain that they would be untrustworthy and freakishly changeable" (IV, 507). While neo-republicans such as Pettit do emphasize the importance of an engaged citizenry and majority rule, there exists in their arguments a tension between this populism and a classical distrust of democratic decision making given the latter's associations with "popular passion, aspirational morality, and sectional interests." See Philip Pettit, "Depoliticizing Democracy," *Ratio Juris* 17, no. 1 (2004): 54. For a sympathetic critique of neo-republicanism's antidemocratic tendencies, see Nadia Urbinati, "Competing for Liberty: The Republican Critique of Democracy," *American Political Science Review* 106, no. 3 (2012): 607–21.

51. As he had in *McCulloch*, Marshall emphasized that while "a state may use many of its acknowledged powers in such manner as to come in conflict with the provisions of the Constitution" and that under such circumstances state law must give way to the Constitution, this principle of sovereignty nonetheless did not "deny the existence of the several powers in the respective governments," such as domestic police powers or the regulation of internal commerce (25 U.S. 352).

52. Marshall's opinion denied that those who conspired to levy war against the United States met the Constitution's standard of treason absent subsequent action, maintaining that "the crime of treason should not be extended by construction to doubtful cases, and that crimes not clearly within the constitutional definition should receive such punishment as the legislature in its wisdom may provide" (8 U.S. 127).

53. In *Gibbons*, Marshall's targets were state-issued monopolies as well as individual actors (22 U.S. 222).

54. Pettit (1997), 132.

55. Moreover, by centering their arguments on general themes of "enslavement and subjection," neo-republican arguments hope to promote an ongoing dialogue on domination that is alive to the new concerns of future generations of citizens. See Pettit (1997), 133, 132. For a critique of neo-republican freedom as "profoundly antimarket," see Gerald F. Gaus, "Backwards Into the Future: Neo-

republicanism as a Postsocialist Critique of Market Society," *Social Philosophy & Policy* 20, no. 1 (2003): 68.

56. Pettit (2012), 111. See also Philip Pettit, "Freedom in the Market," *Politics, Philosophy & Economics* 5, no. 2 (2006): 131–49.

57. See, again, Marshall's opinion in *Gibbons v. Ogden*, which invalidated the "invidious and partial restraints" imposed on commercial intercourse imposed by the Livingston-Fulton steamboat monopoly (22 U.S. 231).

58. On this relationship, consider Richard Dagger, "Neo-Republicanism and the Civic Economy," *Politics, Philosophy & Economics* 5, no. 2 (2006): 151–73; and Eric MacGilvray, *The Invention of Market Freedom* (New York: Cambridge University Press, 2011), 196.

Chapter 4

1. This chapter relies on the terms "Native American" and "American Indian" as the common designations for indigenous peoples in North America during Marshall's lifetime. See the distinctions made by Peter D'Errico in his "John Marshall: Indian Lover?," *Journal of the West* 39, no. 3 (2000): 19–30.

2. For studies of Marshall that reach this conclusion, see, e.g., Corwin (1919), 193–94; Beveridge (1919, IV), 543, 551; Stites (1981), 161–63; Newmyer (2001), 450, 457; Simon (2002), 300; and Unger (2014), 311–12.

3. Charles F. Hobson, "Defining the Office: John Marshall as Chief Justice," *University of Pennsylvania Law Review* 154, no. 6 (2006): 1437.

4. The provenance of the remark is discussed in Anton-Herman Chroust, "Did President Jackson Actually Threaten the Supreme Court of the United States with Nonenforcement of Its Injunction Against the State of Georgia?," *American Journal of Legal History* 4, no. 1 (1960): 76–78.

5. William F. Swindler, "Politics as Law: The Cherokee Cases," *American Indian Law Review* 3, no. 1 (1975): 17.

6. David E. Wilkins argues in his *American Indian Sovereignty and the U.S. Supreme Court: The Masking of Justice* (Austin: University of Texas Press, 1997) that the Marshall Court was engaged in a conniving effort to divest Native Americans of their rights. Similarly, Joseph Burke alleges that Marshall used the Cherokee cases to set up a showdown between the Court and the political branches in his "The Cherokee Cases: A Study in Law, Politics, and Morality," *Stanford Law Review* 21, no. 3 (1969): 510. More charitably, Daniel Walker Howe (2007) has suggested that Marshall was defending the tribes to protect federal treaties and the authority of the national government (121, 282).

7. Thus a recent casebook on federal Indian law states that the Marshall Trilogy provided "foundational principles for guiding the deliberations of Congress and the decisions of courts on the nature of federal powers over tribes, Indian

self-government, issues of jurisdiction in Indian country, and the special rights of tribal Indians as groups." See David H. Getches, Charles F. Wilkinson, and Robert A. Williams, Jr., *Federal Indian Law: Cases and Materials*, 5th ed. (St. Paul, MN: West Group, 2004), 257. See also Matthew L. M. Fletcher, "The Iron Cold of the Marshall Trilogy," *North Dakota Law Review* 82, no. 4 (2006): 627–96. Scholars of federal Indian law have disagreed on the question of whether the logic of Marshall's opinions harmed or helped the Native Americans in the long term. Charles Wilkinson argues that the opinions "conceived a model that can be described broadly as calling for largely autonomous tribal governments subject to an overriding federal authority but essentially free of state control," while legal theorist Robert Williams Jr., flays Marshall for creating a "model of inferior and diminished Indian rights." See Charles F. Wilkinson, *American Indians, Time, and Law: Native Societies in a Modern Constitutional Democracy* (New Haven, CT: Yale University Press, 1987), 24; and Robert A. Williams, *Like a Loaded Weapon: The Rehnquist court, Indian Rights, and the Legal History of Racism in America* (Minneapolis: University of Minnesota Press, 2005), 48–49.

8. Over the years, various scholars have questioned whether the Marshall's Trilogy is the work of a "colonial historian," a "republican schoolmaster," or even an "Indian Lover." See Ralph Lerner, "The Supreme Court as Republican Schoolmaster," in *The Supreme Court Review*, ed. Philip B. Kurland (Chicago: University of Chicago Press, 1967), 128–80; Lindsay G. Robertson, "John Marshall as Colonial Historian: Reconsidering the Origins of the Discovery Doctrine," *Journal of Law & Politics* 13 (1997): 759–77; D'Errico (2000), 19–30; Eric Kades, "History and Interpretation in the Great Case of *Johnson v. M'Intosh*," *Law and History Review* 19, no. 1 (2001): 67–116; and Blake A. Watson, "John Marshall and Indian Land Rights: A Historical Rejoinder to the Claim of 'Universal Recognition' of the Doctrine of Discovery," *Seton Hall Law Review* 36, no. 2 (2006): 481–549.

9. Rennard Strickland notes that many American citizens "thought of these Indian issues and Indian conflict with the states as a 'rehearsal for abolition.'" See his "The Tribal Struggle for Indian Sovereignty: The Story of the *Cherokee Cases*," in *Race Law Stories*, ed. Rachel F. Moran and Devon W. Carbado (New York: Thomson Reuters, 2008), 38. Similarly, Gerard Magliocca, who argues that the memory of the Trail of Tears was an important reference point for those who framed the Fourteenth Amendment, casts the American abolitionist movement as "largely born from the ashes of *Worcester*" in his "Cherokee Removal and the Fourteenth Amendment," *Duke Law Journal* 53, no. 3 (2003): 879.

10. Faulkner (1968), 58. Stites (1981) takes a different approach, claiming that Marshall was the lone voice in the proverbial wilderness urging a policy of "justice and humanity" toward the tribes (160, 162).

11. Richard A. Brisbin, "John Marshall on History, Virtue, and Legality," in Shevory (1989), 95–117.

12. Stephen Breyer, "The Cherokee Indians and the Supreme Court," *Georgia Historical Quarterly* 87, no. 3 (2003): 408–26.

13. A number of scholars have commented on the paradoxical character of nationalism. For example, Shlomo Alvineri describes nationalism as "a two-headed animal," emancipating people based on ideas of freedom and self-determination yet also carrying "the potential of turning xenophobic, intolerant of minorities, repressive of dissent." See his "A Fate Worse Than Communism?," *Jerusalem Post* 8 (1991). Similarly, Jeff Spinner-Halev argues that "nationalism . . . has been both a movement against oppression and a movement that itself oppresses." See his *Boundaries of Citizenship: Race, Ethnicity, and Nationality in the Liberal State* (Baltimore, MD: Johns Hopkins University Press, 1994), 141.

14. Recent histories of the dispossession of Native American land and the Marshall Court's role in this process are found in Stuart Banner, *How the Indians Lost their Land: Law and Power on the Frontier* (Cambridge, MA: Harvard University Press, 2005); and Lindsay Robertson, *Conquest by Law: How the Discovery of America Dispossessed Indigenous Peoples of Their Lands* (New York: Oxford University Press, 2005).

15. According to Kades (2001), there is considerable evidence that *Johnson* was a feigned case whose ulterior purpose was to confirm the real estate titles of the Illinois-Wabash Land Company. Robertson (2005) has gone a step further, arguing that not only was *Johnson* a product of collusion, but also that Marshall himself manipulated the doctrine of discovery to quell anger in Virginia stemming from the Court's earlier decision in *Cohens v. Virginia* (1821), a case that "created a dangerous political rift between the Court and powerful Virginians that the *Johnson* opinion would help close" (78).

16. McIntosh signed his last name with a "c" instead of an apostrophe, but the Supreme Court truncated his name. See Kades (2000), 1068.

17. As Marshall put it, "that discovery gave title to the government by whose subjects, or by whose authority, it was made against all other European governments . . . It was a right with which no Europeans could interfere. It was a right which all asserted for themselves, and to the assertion of which by others all assented" (21 U.S. 573).

18. Steven T. Newcomb, *Pagans in the Promised Land: Decoding the Doctrine of Christian Discovery* (Golden, CO: Fulcrum, 2008), 82–84.

19. Banner (2007), 12, 40.

20. See Robertson (2005), 95–117.

21. See Blake A. Watson, "The Impact of the American Doctrine of Discovery on Native Land Rights in Australia, Canada, and New Zealand," *Seattle University Law Review* 34, no. 2 (2011): 507–51.

22. For example, Stites (1981) argues that land transfers from the Native Americans to the federal government often concealed the practice of "bribery, cajolery, fraud, and outright intimidation" (158).

23. Perhaps the most significant commitment occurred in 1802 when the state of Georgia ceded roughly 35 million acres comprising present-day Mississippi and Alabama—the so-called "Yazoo territory"—in return for money and

a guarantee that Native Americans would be removed peaceably from Georgia lands. See Anthony F. C. Wallace, *The Long, Bitter Trail: Andrew Jackson and the Indians* (New York: Macmillan, 1993), 63. Years later, the title to the Yazoo territory provided the backdrop for Marshall's construction of the contract clause in *Fletcher v. Peck* (1810).

24. See the reconstruction provided in Stites (1981), 157–67.

25. Laura F. Edwards, *A Legal History of the Civil War and Reconstruction: A Nation of Rights* (New York: Cambridge University Press, 2015), 115.

26. This stance grounds Jean Edward Smith's (1996) claim that "only the Court offered the Cherokees an opportunity to preserve their land and their way of life" (516).

27. President Jackson, sensing a chain reaction of defiance to the federal government spreading to the Carolinas, soon pressured Georgia to release Worcester and his fellow missionary, Dr. Elizur Butler. In fact, Georgia's intransigence in the face of the Court's decisions was fodder for Jackson's more aggressive stance on federal authority. Marshall seemed to take a wry satisfaction in Jackson's *volte-face*. Only a few months after *Worcester*, Marshall summed up Southern opinion of Jackson to Joseph Story in these terms: "Imitating the Quaker who said the dog he wished to destroy was gone mad, they said Andrew Jackson had become a Federalist, even an ultra-Federalist. To have said he was ready to break down and trample on every other department of the government would not have injured him, but to say that he was a Federalist—a convert to the opinions of Washington, was a mortal blow under which he is yet staggering" (Fletcher 2006, 641, 644–45).

28. Strickland (2008), 55–56.

29. See Fletcher (2006), 647–48. Justice Antonin Scalia's majority opinion in *Nevada v. Hicks* (2001) epitomizes the lip service given to the Trilogy by the modern Court in noting that "[t]hough tribes are often referred to as 'sovereign' entities, it was 'long ago' that 'the Court departed from Chief Justice Marshall's view that 'the laws of [a State] can have no force' within reservation boundaries'" (533 U.S. 361).

30. Smith (1991), 85–86, 94.

31. Ibid., 14. A separate question, one that need not detain us long here, is whether such shared recollections need be historically accurate. But see the French religious historian Ernest Renan's theory that national identity has depended fundamentally on a people's ability to forget some aspects of their past in his *Qu'est-ce qu'une nation?/What Is a Nation?*, trans. Wanda Romer Taylor (Toronto: Tapir, 1996), 53.

32. Walker Connor, *Ethnonationalism: The Quest for Understanding* (Princeton, NJ: Princeton University Press, 1994), xi.

33. Ibid., 202.

34. See Russell Hardin's discussion of the durability of ethnic identity in his *One for All: The Logic of Group Conflict* (Princeton, NJ: Princeton University Press, 1995), 149.

35. Cynthia H. Enloe, *Ethnic Conflict and Political Development* (Boston, MA: Little, Brown and Co., 1973); Donald L. Horowitz, *Ethnic Groups in Conflict* (Berkeley: University of California Press, 1985); Craig Calhoun, "Nationalism and Ethnicity," *Annual Review of Sociology* 19 (1993): 211–39; and Pierre Manent, *A World Beyond Politics? A Defense of the Nation-State*, trans. Marc LePain (Princeton, NJ: Princeton University Press, 2006).

36. On this point, see Robert J. Schiller, "Weak Economies Foment Ethnic Nationalism," *The New York Times*, October 16, 2016, BU3.

37. According to Stites (1981, 145–48), Marshall owned several slaves during his lifetime, despite (as a Southerner, no less) avowing personal abhorrence for the institution. Unlike Native Americans, Marshall believed that African Americans would never see themselves included within a constitutional nationalism that at least for the short term secured their enslavement. Accordingly, from 1823 until his death he played an active role as president of the Virginia branch of the American Colonization Society, which promoted the voluntary relocation of African Americans to the colony of Liberia in Africa.

38. The Court was badly divided in *Cherokee Nation*, with a total of four opinions written among the seven justices. Although Marshall wrote on behalf of the majority, only John McClean joined his opinion. The concurring opinions of William Johnson and Henry Baldwin were strident defenses of Georgia's sovereignty over Cherokee land. In an otherwise cautious dissent, Justice Smith Thompson (joined by Marshall's longtime ally Story) argued in striking terms "[t]hat the Cherokees compose a foreign state within the sense and meaning of the Constitution, and constitute a competent party of maintain a suit against the State of Georgia" (30 U.S. 80). Having been absent from oral arguments, Justice Gabriel Duvall abstained from the vote.

39. For Berlin's distinction between natural, mild forms of nationalism and its extreme expressions, see his "Nationalism: Past Neglect and Present Power," in *Against the Current: Essays in the History of Ideas*, ed. Henry Hardy (New York: Viking Press, 1980), 333–55.

40. For prominent examples, see Avishai Margalit and Joseph Raz, "National Self-determination," *Journal of Philosophy* 87, no. 9 (1990): 439–61; Yael Tamir, *Liberal Nationalism* (Princeton, NJ: Princeton University Press, 1993); Miller (1995); and Kai Nielsen, "Cultural Nationalism, Neither Ethnic nor Civic," in *Theorizing Nationalism*, ed. Ronald Beiner (Albany: State University of New York Press, 1999), 119–30. Even John Rawls stresses the recognition of the trials and accomplishments of particular cultures as affirming groups' collective "self-respect" in his *Law of Peoples* (Cambridge, MA: Harvard University Press, 1999), 25, 34.

41. Miller (1995), 185.

42. See, e.g., Roger Scruton, "In Defense of Nation," in *Ideas and Politics in Modern Britain*, ed. J. C. D. Clark (London: Macmillan, 1990); Thomas Mertens, "Cosmopolitanism and Citizenship: Kant against Habermas," *European Journal of Philosophy* 4, no. 3 (1996): 193–211; Brian C. J. Singer, "Cultural versus Contractual

Nations: Rethinking their Opposition," *History and Theory* 35, no. 3 (1996): 309–37; Nicholas Xenos, "Civic Nationalism: Oxymoron," *Critical Review* 10, no. 2 (1996): 213–31; and Bernard Yack, "The Myth of the Civic Nation," *Critical Review* 10, no. 2 (1996): 193–211.

43. See Ernst B. Haas, *Nationalism, Liberalism, and Progress: The Rise and Decline of Nationalism* (Ithaca, NY: Cornell University Press, 1997); and Will Kymlicka, *Politics in the Vernacular* (New York: Oxford University Press, 2001), 39–40. In practical terms, these liberal nationalists advocate for group rights and other means for defending ethnic minority cultures. See Siobhan Harty, "The Nation as a Communal Good: A Nationalist Response to the Liberal Conception of Community," *Canadian Journal of Political Science* 32, no. 4 (1999): 665–89. Defining nationalism in more open-ended terms may in fact be the most historically accurate approach. Challenging Smith, Connor, and other ethnonationalist approaches, Linda Colley has argued in her *Britons: Forging the Nation, 1707–1837* (London: Pimlico, 1994) that these plural approaches to understanding national identity are more historically accurate than the arguments of "those who are accustomed to thinking of nations only as historic phenomena characterised by cultural and ethnic homogeneity" (5). According to Colley, most nations in fact "have always been culturally and ethnically diverse, problematic, protean and artificial constructs that take shape very quickly and come apart just as fast."

44. Marshall traces this slow process of subjection in some detail. The Native Americans, "not well acquainted with the exact meaning of words," did not consider it important "whether they were called the subjects or the children of their father in Europe." They grew "lavish in professions of duty and affection, in return for the rich presents they received" and were even "willing to profess dependence on the power which furnished supplies of which they were in absolute need" so long as their internal autonomy remained untouched (31 U.S. 546–47).

45. Marshall quotes a speech by the English superintendent of Indian affairs in 1763, recalling the king's order to his governors and subjects "to treat Indians with justice and humanity, and to forbear all encroachments on the territories allotted to them" (31 U.S. 547).

46. Anderson (2006), esp. 85–114. Striking a similar chord, Anderson's mentor, Eric Hobsbawm, argues that traditions are invented to impose structure and continuity amid constant social change in his "Introduction: Inventing Traditions," in *The Invention of Tradition*, ed. Eric Hobsbawm and Terence Ranger (Cambridge: Cambridge University Press, 1983), 1–14.

47. Ernest Gellner, *Nations and Nationalism* (Ithaca, NY: Cornell University Press, 1983), 6–7. As Gellner notes, "a mere category of persons (say, occupants of a given territory, or speakers of a given language, for example) becomes a nation if and when the members of the category firmly recognize certain mutual rights and duties to each other in virtue of their shared membership of it. It is their recognition of each other as fellows of this kind which turns them into a nation,

and not the other shared attributes, whatever they might be, which separate that category from non-members" (7).

48. Rogers Brubaker, *Nationalism Reframed: Nationhood and the National Question in the New Europe* (New York: Cambridge University Press, 1996); *Ethnicity Without Groups* (Cambridge, MA: Harvard University Press, 2004); and David D. Laitin, *Nations, States, and Violence* (New York: Oxford University Press, 2007).

49. Susan-Mary Grant, "When Was the First New Nation? Locating America in a National Context," in *When Is the Nation? Towards an Understanding of Theories of Nationalism*, ed. Atsuko Ichijo and Gordana Uzelac (London: Routledge, 2005), 173–74. But see some of Walker Connor's early work, which denies nationhood to the United States "in the pristine sense of the word." See his "A Nation Is a Nation, Is a State, Is an Ethnic Group, Is a . . . ," *Ethnic and Racial Studies* 1, no. 4 (1978): 381.

50. Habermas argues that constitutional patriotism entails not the erasure of local attachments, but their criticism and reinterpretation in light of shared general ideas of constitutional democracy. See his "Historical Consciousness and Post-Traditional Identity: The Federal Republic's Orientation to the West," in *The New Conservatism: Cultural Criticism and the Historians' Debate*, trans. and ed. Shierry Weber Nicholson (Cambridge, MA: MIT Press, 1989), 249–67. See also Habermas (1997), 499.

51. Craig J. Calhoun, "Imagining Solidarity: Cosmopolitanism, Constitutional Patriotism, and the Public Sphere," *Public Culture* 14, no. 1 (2002): 147–71; and *Nations Matter* (New York: Routledge, 2007).

52. Müller (2007), 6.

53. Hans Kohn, *American Nationalism: An Interpretive Essay* (New York: Macmillan, 1957), 8.

54. Benjamin Barber, "Constitutional Faith," in Martha Nussbaum, *For Love of Country? Debating the Limits of Patriotism*, ed. Joshua Cohen (Boston, MA: Beacon Press, 2002), 30, 32.

55. Sanford V. Levinson, *Constitutional Faith* (Princeton, NJ: Princeton University Press, 2011), 7, 4. But note Levinson's coda to the 2011 edition of his book, which laments the breakdown of this community in part because of the provisions of the Constitution that frustrate constitutional revision and change (246–55).

56. The petition of the Cherokee had entreated the Court to "interfere" in the actions of the state of Georgia (30 U.S. 10).

57. Nor is it clear what Marshall expected would become of Native Americans in the United States. One indication is provided during his time as a member of the Virginia House of Delegates, where he supported a 1784 bill introduced by Patrick Henry encouraging intermarriage between whites and Native Americans. See Newmyer (2001), 441.

58. Tassel was charged with murdering another Cherokee man, Sanders "Talking Rock" Ford. Despite the fact that the crime occurred on Cherokee land,

Tassel was tried in a county court, found guilty of murder by a jury of twelve white men, and sentenced to death. On behalf of Cherokee Chief John Ross, William Wirt appealed Tassel's sentence to the Supreme Court to suspend Tassel's execution. The Court quickly issued a mandate staying the execution and requesting records of the state trial, orders the state of Georgia predictably ignored.

59. On the danger of national identities that rest on underspecified abstract ideas, see Claes G. Ryn, "Democracy and Nationhood," in *National Identity as an Issue of Knowledge and Morality*, ed. N. V. Chavchavadze, Ghia Nodia, and Paul Peachey (Washington, DC: Paideia, 1994), 97–106.

60. Although they went unheeded at the time, Marshall's opinions in the Trilogy are a stern example of what Mark Graber (2013) has called "constitutional politics," addressing "questions about who belongs to this distinctive people, the identifiable characteristics that determine membership, and what particular purposes and rules are best for this distinctive people" (15).

Summation

1. On this point, see Walter F. Murphy, "Who Shall Interpret the Constitution?," *Review of Politics* 48, no. 3 (1986): 401–23.

2. See, e.g., William N. Eskridge Jr., "Reneging on History? Playing the Court/Congress/President Civil Rights Game," *California Law Review* 79, no. 3 (1991): 613–84; William N. Eskridge Jr., "Overriding Supreme Court Statutory Interpretation Decisions," *Yale Law Journal* 101, no. 2 (1991): 331–455; John A. Ferejohn and Barry Weingast, "Limitation of Statutes: Strategic Statutory Interpretation," *Georgetown Law Journal* 80, no. 3 (1992): 565–82; Jack Knight and Lee Epstein, *The Choices Justices Make* (Washington, DC: CQ Press, 1998); Lee Epstein, Jack Knight, and Andrew D. Martin, "The Supreme Court as a *Strategic* National Policymaker," *Emory Law Journal* 50, no. 2 (2001): 583–611; Georg Vanberg, "Legislative-Judicial Relations: A Game-Theoretic Approach to Constitutional Review," *American Journal of Political Science* 45, no. 2 (2001): 346–61; and James R. Rogers, Roy B. Flemming, and Jon R. Bond, eds., *Institutional Games and the U.S. Supreme Court* (Charlottesville: University of Virginia Press, 2006).

3. William James Booth, *Communities of Memory: On Witness, Identity, and Injustice* (Ithaca, NY: Cornell University Press, 2006), 56.

4. John Marshall, "Marshall to Story, 25 December 1832," in *The Papers of John Marshall*, 12 vols., ed. Charles F. Hobson (Chapel Hill: University of North Carolina Press, 2006), XII: 247.

5. The concept of constitutional failure is best articulated by Sotirios A. Barber in his *Constitutional Failure* (Lawrence: University Press of Kansas, 2014). Barber characterizes constitutional breakdown as "less an institutional than an attitudinal matter," maintaining that "constitutional survival in America depends

on attitudes like patriotism, trust, and magnanimity, and that relying mainly on checking and balancing self-serving attitudes guarantees eventual constitutional failure" (2). However, Marshall would part ways with Barber's veneration of the act of the founders rather than the Constitution they produced (18–20).

Bibliography

Ackerman, Bruce. "Constitutional Politics/Constitutional Law." *Yale Law Review* 99, no. 3 (1989), 453–547.

———. *We the People: Foundations*. Cambridge, MA: Harvard University Press, 1991.

———. *We the People: Transformations*. Cambridge, MA: Harvard University Press, 1998.

———. "The Living Constitution." *Harvard Law Review* 120, no. 7 (2007): 1737–812.

———. *We the People: The Civil Rights Revolution*. Cambridge, MA: Harvard University Press, 2014.

Adair, Douglass. " 'That Politics May Be Reduced to a Science': David Hume, James Madison and the Tenth Federalist." *Huntington Library Quarterly* 20, no. 4 (1957): 343–60.

Agresto, John T. "Liberty, Virtue, and Republicanism: 1776–1787." *Review of Politics* 39, no. 4 (1977): 473–504.

Alexander, Larry, and Frederick Schauer. "On Extrajudicial Constitutional Interpretation." *Harvard Law Review* 110, no. 7 (1997): 1359–87.

———. "Defending Judicial Supremacy: A Reply." *Constitutional Commentary* 17, no. 3 (2000): 455–82.

Allen, W. B., and Gordon Lloyd, eds. *The Essential Antifederalist*. Lanham, MD: Rowman and Littlefield, 2002.

Alstyne, William W. Van. "A Critical Guide to *Marbury v. Madison*." *Duke Law Journal* 18, no. 1 (1969): 1–47.

Alvineri, Shlomo. "A Fate Worse Than Communism?" *Jerusalem Post*, September 8, 1991.

Amar, Akhil Reed. "Marbury, Section 13, and the Original Jurisdiction of the Supreme Court." *University of Chicago Law Review* 56, no. 2 (1989): 443–99.

———. "Popular Sovereignty and Constitutional Amendment." In *Responding to Imperfection: The Theory and Practice of Constitutional Amendment*, edited by Sanford V. Levinson, 89–116. Princeton, NJ: Princeton University Press, 1995.

Anderson, Benedict. *Imagined Communities*. New York: Verso, 2006.

Appleby, Joyce. "The Social Origins of American Revolutionary Ideology." *The Journal of American History* 64, no. 4 (1978): 935–58.

———. *Capitalism and a New Social Order: The Republican Vision of the 1790s.* New York: New York University Press, 1984.

———. "Republicanism and Ideology." *American Quarterly* 37, no. 4 (1985): 461–73.

———. *Liberalism and Republicanism in the Historical Imagination.* Cambridge, MA: Harvard University Press, 1992.

Bailyn, Bernard. *The Ideological Origins of the American Revolution.* Cambridge, MA: Harvard University Press, 1967.

———. "Toward a Republican Synthesis: The Emergence of an Understanding of Republicanism in American Historiography." *William and Mary Quarterly* 29, no. 1 (1972): 49–80.

Baker, Jonathan B. "Has The Contract Clause Counter-Revolution Halted? Rhetoric, Rights, and Markets in Constitutional Analysis." *Hastings Constitutional Law Quarterly* 12, no. 1 (1984): 17–104.

Baker, Leonard. *John Marshall: A Life in Law.* New York: Macmillan, 1974.

Balkin, Jack M. *Living Originalism.* Cambridge, MA: Harvard University Press, 2011.

Banner, Stuart. *How the Indians Lost Their Land: Law and Power on the Frontier.* Cambridge, MA: Harvard University Press, 2005.

Banning, Lance. "Republican Ideology and the Triumph of the Constitution." *William and Mary Quarterly* 31, no. 2 (1974): 167–88.

———. *The Jeffersonian Persuasion: Evolution of a Party Ideology.* Ithaca, NY: Cornell University Press, 1978.

Barber, Benjamin R. "Constitutional Faith." In Martha C. Nussbaum, *For Love of Country? Debating the Limits of Patriotism*, edited by Joshua Cohen, 30–37. Boston, MA: Beacon Press, 1996.

Barber, Sotirios A. *The Fallacies of States' Rights.* Cambridge, MA: Harvard University Press, 2013.

———. *Constitutional Failure.* Lawrence, KS: University Press of Kansas, 2014.

Barber, Sotirios A., and James E. Fleming. *Constitutional Interpretation: The Basic Questions.* New York: Oxford University Press, 2007.

Barker, Rodney. *Legitimating Identities: The Self-Presentations of Rulers and Subjects.* Cambridge: Cambridge University Press, 2001.

Barnett, Randy E. "Constitutional Legitimacy." *Columbia Law Review* 103, no. 1 (2003): 111–48.

———. *Restoring the Lost Constitution.* Princeton, NJ: Princeton University Press, 2004.

Belz, Herman, Ronald Hoffman, and Peter J. Albert, eds. *To Form a More Perfect Union: The Critical Ideas of the Constitution.* Charlottesville, VA: University of Virginia Press, 1992.

Bennett, Walter. *American Theories of Federalism.* Tuscaloosa, AL: University of Alabama Press, 1964.

Berlin, Isaiah. "Nationalism: Past Neglect and Present Power." In *Against the Current: Essays in the History of Ideas*, edited by Henry Hardy, 333–55. New York: Viking Press, 1980.

———. "Two Concepts of Liberty." In *Four Essays on Liberty*, by Isaiah Berlin, 118–72. Oxford: Oxford University Press, 1992.

Berthoff, Rowland. "Independence and Attachment, Virtue and Interest: From Republican Citizen to Free Enterpriser, 1787–1837." In *Uprooted Americans: Essays in Honor of Oscar Handlin*, edited by Richard L. Bushman, Neil Harris, David Rothman, Barbara Miller Solomon, and Stephen Thernstrom, 99–124. Boston, MA: Little, Brown and Co., 1979.

Beveridge, Albert J. *The Life of John Marshall*. 4 vols. Boston and New York: Houghton Mifflin, 1919.

Bickel, Alexander M. *The Least Dangerous Branch: The Supreme Court at the Bar of Politics*. Indianapolis, IN: Bobbs-Merrill, 1962.

Bloch, Susan Low, and Maeva Marcus. "John Marshall's Selective Use of History in *Marbury v. Madison*." *Wisconsin Law Review* 301, no. 2 (1986): 301–37.

Bloom Jr., Lackland H. *Do Great Cases Make Bad Law?* New York: Oxford University Press, 2014.

Bogen, David S. "The Scandal of Smith and Buchanan: The Skeletons in the *McCulloch v. Maryland* Closet." *Maryland Law Forum* 9, no. 4 (1985): 125–32.

Booth, William James. *Communities of Memory: On Witness, Identity, and Injustice*. Ithaca, NY: Cornell University Press, 2006.

Bork, Robert H. *Coercing Virtue: The Worldwide Rule of Judges*. Washington: AEI Press, 2003.

Breyer, Stephen. "The Cherokee Indians and the Supreme Court." *Georgia Historical Quarterly* 87, no. 3 (2003): 408–26.

Brisben, Richard A. "John Marshall and the Nature of Law in the Early Republic." *The Virginia Magazine of History and Biography* 98, no. 1 (1990): 57–80.

Brubaker, Rogers. *Nationalism Reframed: Nationhood and the National Question in the New Europe*. New York: Cambridge University Press, 1996.

———. *Ethnicity Without Groups*. Cambridge, MA: Harvard University Press, 2004.

Buel Jr., Richard. "Democracy and the American Revolution: A Frame of Reference." *William and Mary Quarterly* 21, no. 2 (1964): 165–90.

Burke, Joseph. "The Cherokee Cases: A Study in Law, Politics, and Morality." *Stanford Law Review* 21, no. 3 (1969): 500–31.

Calhoun, Craig J. "Nationalism and Ethnicity." *Annual Review of Sociology* 19 (1993): 211–39.

———. "Imagining Solidarity: Cosmopolitanism, Constitutional Patriotism, and the Public Sphere." *Public Culture* 14, no. 1 (2002): 147–71.

———. *Nations Matter*. New York: Routledge, 2007.

Campbell, A. I. L. " 'It Is a *Constitution* We Are Expounding': Chief Justice Marshall and the 'Necessary and Proper' Clause." *Journal of Legal History* 12, no. 3 (1991): 190–245.

Cardozo, Benjamin N. *The Nature of the Judicial Process*. New Haven, CT: Yale University Press, 1921.

Carey, John M. "Parchment, Equilibria, and Institutions." *Comparative Political Studies* 33, no. 6/7 (2000): 735–61.

Chroust, Anton-Herman. "Did President Jackson Actually Threaten the Supreme Court of the United States with Nonenforcement of Its Injunction Against the State of Georgia?" *American Journal of Legal History* 4, no. 1 (1960): 76–78.

Clinton, Robert Lawry. *Marbury v. Madison and Judicial Review*. Lawrence, KS: University Press of Kansas, 1989.

Colley, Linda. *Britons: Forging the Nation, 1707–1837*. London: Pimlico, 1994.

Connor, Walker. "A Nation Is a Nation, Is a State, Is an Ethnic Group, Is a . . . ," *Ethnic and Racial Studies* 1, no. 4 (1978): 377–400.

———. *Ethnonationalism: The Quest for Understanding*. Princeton, NJ: Princeton University Press, 1994.

Copp, David. "The Idea of a Legitimate State." *Philosophy & Public Affairs* 28, no. 1 (1999): 3–45.

Corwin, Edward S. "*Marbury v. Madison* and the Doctrine of Judicial Review." *Michigan Law Review* 12, no. 7 (1914): 538–72.

———. *John Marshall and the Constitution*. New Haven, CT: Yale University Press, 1919.

Costa, Victoria M. "Neo-Republicanism, Freedom as Non-Domination, and Citizen Virtue." *Politics, Philosophy & Economics* 8, no. 4 (2009): 401–19.

Currie, David P. "The Constitution in the Supreme Court: The Powers of the Federal Courts, 1801–1835." *University of Chicago Law Review* 49, no. 4 (1982): 646–724.

D'Errico, Peter. "John Marshall: Indian Lover?" *Journal of the West* 39, no. 3 (2000): 19–30.

Dagger, Richard. "Autonomy, Domination, and the Republican Challenge to Liberalism." In *Autonomy and the Challenges to Liberalism: New Essays*, edited by John Christman and Joel Anderson, 177–203. Cambridge: Cambridge University Press, 2005.

———. "Neo-Republicanism and the Civic Economy." *Politics, Philosophy & Economics* 5, no. 2 (2006): 151–73.

Diggins, John P. *The Lost Soul of American Politics: Virtue, Self-Interest, and the Foundations of Liberalism*. Chicago: University of Chicago Press, 1984.

Dodd, William E. "Chief Justice Marshall and Virginia, 1813–1821." *American Historical Review* 12, no. 4 (1907): 776–87.

Dworetz, Steven M. *The Unvarnished Doctrine: Locke, Liberalism, and the American Revolution*. Durham, NC: Duke University Press, 1990.

Dworkin, Ronald. *Freedom's Law: The Moral Reading of the Constitution*. Cambridge, MA: Harvard University Press, 1996.

———. *Taking Rights Seriously*. London: Bloomsbury, 2013.

Edwards, Laura F. *A Legal History of the Civil War and Reconstruction: A Nation of Rights*. New York: Cambridge University Press, 2015.

Eisgruber, Christopher L. "John Marshall's Judicial Rhetoric." *The Supreme Court Review* (1996): 439–81.

Ellis, Richard. *Aggressive Nationalism: McCulloch v. Maryland and the Foundation of Federal Authority in the Young Republic.* New York: Oxford University Press, 2007.

Elster, Jon. *Ulysses and the Sirens: Studies in Rationality and Irrationality.* Cambridge: Cambridge University Press, 1984.

———. *Ulysses Unbound: Studies in Rationality, Precommitment, and Constraints.* Cambridge: Cambridge University Press, 2000.

Elster, Jon, and Rune Slagstad, eds. *Constitutionalism and Democracy.* New York: Cambridge University Press, 1988.

Ely Jr., James W. "The Marshall Court and Property Rights: A Reappraisal." *John Marshall Law Review* 33, no. 4 (2000): 1023–61.

Enloe, Cynthia H. *Ethnic Conflict and Political Development.* Boston, MA: Little, Brown and Co., 1973.

Epstein, Lee, and Thomas G. Walker. *Constitutional Law for a Changing America.* 9th ed. Los Angeles: CQ Press, 2015.

Epstein, Lee, Jack Knight, and Andrew D. Martin. "The Supreme Court as a Strategic National Policymaker." *Emory Law Journal* 50, no. 2 (2001): 583–611.

Epstein, Richard A. *Takings: Private Property and the Power of Eminent Domain.* Cambridge, MA: Harvard University Press, 1985.

———. *The Classical Liberal Constitution.* Cambridge, MA: Harvard University Press, 2014.

Eskridge, William. "Overriding Supreme Court Statutory Interpretation Decisions." *Yale Law Journal* 101, no. 2 (1991): 331–455.

———. "Reneging on History? Playing the Court/Congress/President Civil Rights Game." *California Law Review* 79, no. 3 (1991): 613–84.

Eskridge, William, and Gary Peller. "The New Public Law Movement: Moderation as a Postmodern Cultural Form." *Michigan Law Review* 89, no. 4 (1991): 707–91.

Fallon Jr., Richard H. *Implementing the Constitution.* Cambridge, MA: Harvard University Press, 2001.

———. "Legitimacy and the Constitution." *Harvard Law Review* 118, no. 6 (2005): 1787–853.

Farber, Daniel A. "The Story of *McCulloch*: Banking on National Power." In *Constitutional Law Stories*, edited by Michael C. Dorf, 34–67. New York: Foundation Press, 2004.

Faulkner, Robert K. *John Marshall's Jurisprudence.* Princeton, NJ: Princeton University Press, 1968.

Ferejohn, John A., and Barry Weingast. "Limitation of Statutes: Strategic Statutory Interpretation." *Georgetown Law Journal* 80, no. 3 (1992): 565–82.

Fiss, Owen M. "Groups and the Equal Protection Clause." *Philosophy & Public Affairs* 5, no. 2 (1976): 107–77.

Flaherty, Martin S. "John Marshall, *McCulloch v. Maryland*, and 'We the People': Revisions in Need of Revising." *William and Mary Law Review* 43, no. 4 (2002): 1339–97.

Fleming, James E. "Fidelity, Change, and the Good Constitution." *American Journal of Comparative Law* 62, no. 3 (2014): 515–45.

Fletcher, Matthew L. M. "The Iron Cold of the Marshall Trilogy." *North Dakota Law Review* 82, no. 4 (2006): 627–96.

Frank, Jason. *Constituent Moments*. Durham, NC: Duke University Press, 2010.

Friedrich, Carl J. *Constitutional Government and Democracy*. Boston, MA: Little, Brown and Co., 1941.

Frisch, Morton J. "John Marshall's Philosophy of Constitutional Republicanism." *Review of Politics* 20, no. 1 (1958): 34–45.

Fritz, Christian G. *American Sovereigns: The People and America's Constitutional Tradition Before the Civil War*. New York: Cambridge University Press, 2008.

Gaus, Gerald F. "Backwards Into The Future: Neorepublicanism as a Postsocialist Critique of Market Society." *Social Philosophy & Policy* 20, no. 1 (2003): 59–91.

Gellner, Ernest. *Nations and Nationalism*. Ithaca, NY: Cornell University Press, 1983.

Getches, David H., Charles F. Wilkinson, and Robert A. Williams Jr., eds. *Federal Indian Law: Cases and Materials*. 5th ed. St. Paul, MN: West Group, 2004.

Goldstein, Leslie Friedman. "Popular Sovereignty, the Origins of Judicial Review, and the Revival of Unwritten Law." *Journal of Politics* 48, no. 1 (1986): 51–71.

Goldstone, Lawrence. *The Activist: John Marshall, Marbury v. Madison, and the Myth of Judicial Review*. New York: Walker and Company, 2008.

Graber, Mark A. "Establishing Judicial Review: *Marbury* and the Judicial Act of 1789." *Tulsa Law Review* 38, no. 4 (2003): 609–50.

———. *A New Introduction to American Constitutionalism*. New York: Oxford University Press, 2013.

Grant, Susan-Mary. "When Was the First New Nation?" In *When is the Nation? Towards an Understanding of Theories of Nationalism*, edited by Atsuko Ichijo and Gordana Uzelac, 157–76. London: Routledge, 2005.

Greene, Jack P. *Peripheries and Center: Constitutional Development in the Extended Polities of the British Empire and the United States, 1607–1788*. Athens: University of Georgia Press, 1986.

———, ed. *The American Revolution: Its Character and Limits*. New York: New York University Press, 1987.

Griffin, Stephen M. *American Constitutionalism: From Theory to Politics*. Princeton, NJ: Princeton University Press, 1996.

Gunnell, John G. *Imagining the American Polity: Political Science and the Discourse of Democracy*. University Park: Penn State University Press, 2004.

Gunther, Gerald, ed. *John Marshall's Defense of McCulloch v. Maryland*. Stanford, CA: Stanford University Press, 1989.

Haas, Ernst B. *Nationalism, Liberalism, and Progress: The Rise and Decline of Nationalism.* Ithaca, NY: Cornell University Press, 1997.

Habermas, Jürgen. *Communication and the Evolution of Society.* Translated by Thomas McCarthy. Boston, MA: Beacon Press, 1979.

———. "Historical Consciousness and Post-Traditional Identity: The Federal Republic's Orientation to the West." In *The New Conservatism: Cultural Criticism and the Historians' Debate,* translated and edited by Shierry Weber Nicholson. Cambridge, MA: MIT Press, 1989.

———. *Between Facts and Norms: Contributions to a Discourse Theory of Democracy.* Translated by William Rehg. Cambridge, MA: Polity Press, 1997.

Haines, Charles G. *The Role of the Supreme Court in American Government and Politics, 1789–1835.* New York: Russell & Russell, 1960.

Hamilton, Alexander. *The Papers of Alexander Hamilton.* 27 vols. Edited by Harold C. Syrett and Jacob E. Cook. New York: Columbia University Press, 1961–1987.

Hamilton, Alexander, James Madison, and John Jay. *The Federalist.* Edited by J. R. Pole. Indianapolis, IN: Hackett, 2005.

Hardin, Russell. *One for All: The Logic of Group Conflict.* Princeton, NJ: Princeton University Press, 1995.

Harty, Siobhan. "The Nation as a Communal Good: A Nationalist Response to the Liberal Conception of Community." *Canadian Journal of Political Science* 32, no. 4 (1999): 665–89.

Hartz, Louis. *The Liberal Tradition in America.* New York: Harvest, 1991.

Hawkins, Michael Daly. "John Marshall Through the Eyes of an Admirer: John Quincy Adams." *William & Mary Law Review* 43, no. 4 (2002): 1453–61.

Hayek, Friedrich A. *The Constitution of Liberty.* Chicago: University of Chicago Press, 2011.

Hirsch, Harry N. *A Theory of Liberty: The Constitution and Minorities.* New York: Routledge, 1992.

Hobsbawm, Eric. "Introduction: Inventing Traditions." In *The Invention of Tradition,* edited by Eric Hobsbawm and Terence Ranger, 1–14. Cambridge: Cambridge University Press, 1983.

Hobson, Charles F. *The Great Chief Justice: John Marshall and the Rule of Law.* Lawrence: University Press of Kansas, 1996.

———. "Defining the Office: John Marshall as Chief Justice." *University of Pennsylvania Law Review* 154, no. 6 (2006): 1421–61.

Hofstadter, Richard. *The American Political Tradition and the Men Who Made It.* New York: Vintage, 1989.

Holmes, Oliver Wendell. *Collected Legal Papers.* New York: Harcourt, Brace, and Howe, 1920.

Holmes, Stephen. *Passions and Constraints.* Chicago: University of Chicago Press, 1995.

Horowitz, Donald L. *Ethnic Groups in Conflict*. Berkeley: University of California Press, 1985.

Howe, Daniel Walker. *What Hath God Wrought: The Transformation of America, 1815–1848*. New York: Oxford University Press, 2007.

Irons, Peter. *A People's History of the Supreme Court*. New York: Viking, 1999.

Jefferson, Thomas. *Jefferson: Political Writings*. Edited by Joyce Appleby and Terence Ball. New York: Cambridge University Press, 1999.

Johnsen, Dawn K. "Functional Departmentalism and Nonjudicial Interpretation: Who Determines Constitutional Meaning?" *Law and Contemporary Problems* 67, no. 3 (2004): 105–48.

Kades, Eric. "History and Interpretation in the Great Case of *Johnson v. M'Intosh*." *Law and History Review* 19, no. 1 (2001): 67–116.

Kahn, Paul W. *The Reign of Law: Marbury v. Madison and the Construction of America*. New Haven, CT: Yale University Press, 2002.

Kalmo, Hent, and Quentin Skinner, eds. *Sovereignty in Fragments: The Past, Present and Future of a Contested Concept*. New York: Cambridge University Press, 2010.

Kalyvas, Andreas, and Ira Katznelson. *Liberal Beginnings: Making a Republic for the Moderns*. New York: Cambridge University Press, 2008.

Kelsen, Hans. *An Introduction to the Problems of Legal Theory*. Translated by Bonnie Litschewski Paulson and Stanley L. Paulson. Oxford: Clarendon, 1992.

Kenyon, Cecelia M. "Republicanism and Radicalism in the American Revolution: An Old Fashioned Interpretation." *William and Mary Quarterly* 19, no. 2 (1962): 153–82.

Killenbeck, Mark R. *McCulloch v. Maryland: Securing a Nation*. Lawrence: University Press of Kansas, 2006.

Kingdon, John W. *America the Unusual*. Belmont, CA: Wadsworth, 1999.

Klarman, Michael J. "How Great Were the 'Great' Marshall Court Decisions?" *Virginia Law Review* 87, no. 6 (2001): 1111–84.

Knight, Jack, and Lee Epstein. *The Choices Justices Make*. Washington, DC: CQ Press, 1998.

Kohn, Hans. *American Nationalism: An Interpretive Essay*. New York: Macmillan, 1957.

Konefsky, Samuel J. *John Marshall and Alexander Hamilton: Architects of the American Constitution*. New York: Macmillan, 1964.

Kramer, Larry D. "The Supreme Court 2000 Term—Foreword: We the Court." *Harvard Law Review* 115 (2001): 4–169.

Kymlicka, Will. *Politics in the Vernacular: Nationalism, Multiculturalism, and Citizenship*. New York: Oxford University Press, 2001.

LaCroix, Alison L. *The Ideological Origins of American Federalism*. Cambridge, MA: Harvard University Press, 2010.

Laitin, David D. *Nations, States, and Violence*. New York: Oxford University Press, 2007.

Lerner, Max. "John Marshall and the Campaign of History." *Columbia Law Review* 39, no. 3 (1939): 396–431.

Lerner, Ralph. "The Supreme Court as Republican Schoolmaster." In *The Supreme Court Review*, edited by Philip B. Kurland, 128–80. Chicago: University of Chicago Press, 1967.

———. "Commerce and Character: The Anglo-American as New-Model Man." *William and Mary Quarterly* 36, no. 1 (1979): 3–26.

———. *The Thinking Revolutionary: Principle and Practice in the New Republic.* Ithaca, NY: Cornell University Press, 1987.

Levinson, Sanford V. "Why I Do Not Teach *Marbury* (Except to Eastern Europeans) and Why You Shouldn't Either." *Wake Forest Law Review* 38 (2002): 553–78.

———. *Constitutional Faith.* Princeton, NJ: Princeton University Press, 2011.

Lewis, William Draper. *Great American Lawyers.* 4 vols. Philadelphia: John C. Winston Co., 1907.

Locke, John. *Second Treatise of Government.* Edited by C. B. Macpherson. Indianapolis, IN: Hackett, 1980.

Lutz, Donald S. "The Theory of Consent in Early State Constitutions." *Publius* 9, no. 2 (1979): 11–42.

Lynch, Joseph M. "*McCulloch v. Maryland*: A Matter of Money Supply." *Seton Hall Law Review* 18, no. 2 (1988): 223–329.

MacGilvray, Eric. *The Invention of Market Freedom.* New York: Cambridge University Press, 2011.

Magliocca, Gerard. "Cherokee Removal and the Fourteenth Amendment." *Duke Law Journal* 53, no. 3 (2003): 875–965.

Manent, Pierre. *A World Beyond Politics? A Defense of the Nation-State.* Translated by Marc LePain. Princeton, NJ: Princeton University Press, 2006.

Margalit, Avishai, and Jacob Raz. "National Self-Determination." *Journal of Philosophy* 87, no. 9 (1990): 439–61.

Marshall, John. *Life of George Washington.* 5 vols. Philadelphia: C.P. Wayne, 1804–1807.

———. *The Papers of John Marshall.* 12 vols. Edited by Charles F. Hobson. Chapel Hill: University of North Carolina Press, 1974–2006.

Matthews, Richard K. *The Radical Politics of Thomas Jefferson: A Revisionist View.* Lawrence: University Press of Kansas, 1984.

———. *If Men Were Angels: James Madison and the Heartless Empire of Reason.* Lawrence: University Press of Kansas, 1995.

Maynor, John W. *Republicanism in the Modern World.* Cambridge, MA: Polity Press, 2003.

McCloskey, Robert G. *The American Supreme Court.* 5th ed. Chicago: University of Chicago Press, 2010.

McCoy, Drew R. *The Elusive Republic: Political Economy in Jeffersonian America.* Chapel Hill: University of North Carolina Press, 1980.

McDonald, Forrest. *Rights and the Union: Imperium in Imperio, 1776–1876.* Lawrence: University Press of Kansas, 2000.

McDowell, Gary. *The Language of Law and the Foundations of American Constitutionalism.* New York: Cambridge University Press, 2010.

Mertens, Thomas. "Cosmopolitanism and Citizenship: Kant against Habermas." *European Journal of Philosophy* 4, no. 3 (1996): 193–211.

Michelman, Frank I. "IDA's Way: Constructing the Respect-Worthy Governmental System." *Fordham Law Review* 72, no. 3 (2003): 345–65.

———. "Is the Constitution a Contract for Legitimacy?" *Review of Constitutional Studies* 8, no. 2 (2003): 101–28.

Miller, David. *On Nationality.* New York: Oxford University Press, 1995.

Miller, Perry. "From the Covenant to the Revival." In *Religion in American Life: The Shaping of American Religion*, edited by James Ward Smith and A. Leland Jamison, 4 vols., 322–68. Princeton, NJ: Princeton University Press, 1961.

Miller, Stephen. "Adam Smith and the Commercial Republic." *Public Interest* 61 (1980): 106–22.

Morgan, Edmund S. *Inventing the People: The Rise of Popular Sovereignty in England and America.* New York: Norton, 1988.

Müller, Jan-Werner. *Constitutional Patriotism.* Princeton, NJ: Princeton University Press, 2007.

———. "A European Constitutional Patriotism? The Case Restated." *European Law Journal* 14, no. 5 (2008): 542–57.

Murphy, Walter F. "Who Shall Interpret the Constitution?" *Review of Politics* 48, no. 3 (1986): 401–23.

Murrin, John. "The Great Inversion, or Court versus Country: A Comparison of the Revolution Settlements in England (1688–1721), and America (1776–1816)." In *Three British Revolutions: 1641, 1688, 1776*, edited by J. G. A. Pocock, 368–453. Princeton, NJ: Princeton University Press, 1980.

———. "A Roof Without Walls: The Dilemma of American National Identity." In *Beyond Confederation: Origins of The Constitution and American National Identity*, edited by Richard Beeman, Stephen Botein, and Edward C. Carter Jr., 333–48. Chapel Hill: University of North Carolina Press, 1987.

———. "Self-Interest Conquers Patriotism: Republicans, Liberals, and Indians Reshape the Nation." In *The American Revolution: Its Character and Limits*, edited by Jack P. Greene, 224–29. New York: New York University Press, 1987.

Nagel, Thomas. *Equality and Partiality.* New York: Oxford University Press, 1991.

Nelson, William E. "The Eighteenth-Century Background of John Marshall's Constitutional Jurisprudence." *Michigan Law Review* 76 (1978): 893–960.

Newcomb, Steven T. *Pagans in the Promised Land: Decoding the Doctrine of Christian Discovery.* Golden, CO: Fulcrum, 2008.

Newmyer, R. Kent. "John Marshall, *McCulloch v. Maryland*, and the Southern States' Rights Tradition." *John Marshall Law Review* 33, no. 4 (2000): 875–934.

———. *John Marshall and the Heroic Age of the Supreme Court.* Baton Rouge: Louisiana State University Press, 2001.

Nielsen, Kai. "Cultural Nationalism, Neither Ethnic nor Civic." In *Theorizing Nationalism*, edited by Ronald Beiner, 119–30. Albany: State University of New York Press, 1999.

O'Fallon, James M. "Marbury." *Stanford Law Review* 44, no. 2 (1992): 219–60.

Olken, Samuel R. "John Marshall and Spencer Roane: An Historical Analysis of the Conflict over U.S. Supreme Court Appellate Jurisdiction." *Journal of Supreme Court History* 14 (1990): 125–41.

Orren, Karen, and Christopher Walker. "Cold Case File: Indictable Acts and Officer Accountability in *Marbury v. Madison.*" *American Political Science Review* 107, no. 2 (2013): 241–58.

Pangle, Thomas L. *The Spirit of Modern Republicanism: The Moral Vision of the American Founders and the Philosophy of Locke.* Chicago: University of Chicago Press, 1988.

Parrington, Vernon Louis. *Main Currents in American Thought: The Romantic Revolution in America, 1800–1860.* New York: Harcourt, Brace and Co., 1927.

Paul, John Richard. *Without Precedent: Chief Justice John Marshall and His Times.* New York: Penguin, 2018.

Pettit, Philip. *Republicanism: A Theory of Freedom and Government.* Oxford: Clarendon Press, 1997.

———. *A Theory of Freedom: The Psychology and Politics of Agency.* Oxford: Oxford University Press, 2001.

———. "Depoliticizing Democracy." *Ratio Juris* 17, no. 1 (2004): 52–65.

———. "Freedom in the Market." *Politics, Philosophy & Economics* 5, no. 2 (2006): 131–49.

———. *On The People's Terms: A Republican Theory and Model of Democracy.* New York: Cambridge University Press, 2013.

———. "Two Republican Traditions." In *Republican Democracy: Liberty, Law, and Politics*, edited by Andreas Niederberger and Philipp Schink, 169–204. Edinburgh: Edinburgh University Press, 2013.

———. *Just Freedom.* New York: Norton, 2014.

Plous, Harold J., and Gordon E. Baker. "*McCulloch v. Maryland*: Right Principle, Wrong Case." *Stanford Law Review* 9, no. 4 (1957): 710–30.

Pocock, J. G. A. *The Machiavellian Moment: Florentine Political Thought and the Atlantic Republican Tradition.* Princeton, NJ: Princeton University Press, 1975.

———. "Virtues, Rights, and Manners: A Model for Historians of Political Thought." *Political Theory* 9, no. 3 (1981): 353–68.

Podoksik, Efraim. "One Concept of Liberty: Toward Writing the History of a Political Concept." *Journal of the History of Ideas* 71, no. 2 (2010): 219–40.

Prest, Wilfrid. *William Blackstone: Law and Letters in the Eighteenth Century.* New York: Oxford University Press, 2008.

Przeworski, Adam. *Sustainable Democracy*. New York: Cambridge University Press, 1995.

Rahe, Paul A. *Republics Ancient and Modern: Classical Republicanism and the American Revolution*. Chapel Hill: University of North Carolina Press, 1992.

Rakove, Jack N. "The Origins of Judicial Review: A Plea for New Contexts." *Stanford Law Review* 49, no. 5 (1997): 1031–64.

Rawls, John. *The Law of Peoples*. Cambridge, MA: Harvard University Press, 1999.

———. *Political Liberalism*. New York: Columbia University Press, 2003.

Raz, Joseph. "On the Authority and Interpretation of Constitutions: Some Preliminaries." In *Constitutionalism: Philosophical Foundations*, edited by Larry Alexander, 152–93. New York: Cambridge University Press, 2001.

Reid, John Phillip. *The Concept of Liberty in the Age of the American Revolution*. Chicago: University of Chicago Press, 1988.

Remini, Robert V. *Andrew Jackson and the Bank War*. New York: Norton, 1967.

Renan, Ernest. *Qu'est-ce qu'une nation?/What Is a Nation?* Translated by Wanda Romer Taylor. Toronto: Tapir Press, 1996.

Riemer, Neal. "The Republicanism of James Madison." *Political Science Quarterly* 69, no. 1 (1954): 45–64.

Robbins, Caroline. *The Eighteenth-Century Commonwealthman: Studies in the Transmission, Development, and Circumstance of English Liberal Thought from the Restoration of Charles II until the War with the Thirteen Colonies*. Cambridge, MA: Harvard University Press, 1967.

Robertson, Lindsay G. "John Marshall as Colonial Historian: Reconsidering the Origins of the Discovery Doctrine." *Journal of Law & Politics* 13 (1997): 759–77.

———. *Conquest by Law: How the Discovery of America Dispossessed Indigenous Peoples of Their Lands*. New York: Oxford University Press, 2005.

Rodgers, Daniel T. "Republicanism: The Career of a Concept." *Journal of American History* 79, no. 1 (1992): 11–38.

Rogers, James R., Roy B. Flemming, and Jon R. Bond, eds. *Institutional Games and the U.S. Supreme Court*. Charlottesville: University of Virginia Press, 2006.

Rossiter, Clinton. *Seedtime of the Republic*. New York: Harcourt, Brace and Co., 1953.

Ryn, Claes G. "Democracy and Nationhood." In *National Identity as an Issue of Knowledge and Morality*, edited by N. V. Chavchavadze, Ghia Nodia, and Paul Peachey, 97–106. Washington, DC: Paideia, 1994.

Savelsberg, Joachim J. "Cultures of Control in Contemporary Societies." *Law and Social Inquiry* 27, no. 3 (2002): 685–710.

Schiller, Robert J. "Weak Economies Foment Ethnic Nationalism." *The New York Times*, October 16, 2016, BU3.

Schmitt, Carl. *Constitutional Theory*. Durham, NC: Duke University Press, 2008.

Schwartz, David S. "Misreading *McCulloch v. Maryland*." *Journal of Constitutional Law* 18, no. 1 (2015): 1–94.

Scruton, Roger. "In Defense of Nation." In *Ideas and Politics in Modern Britain*, edited by J. C. D. Clark, 53–86. London: Macmillan, 1990.

Shallhope, Robert. "Toward a Republican Synthesis: The Emergence of an Understanding of Republicanism in American Historiography." *William and Mary Quarterly* 29, no. 1 (1972): 49–80.

Sheehan, Colleen A., and Gary L. McDowell, eds. *Friends of the Constitution: Writings of the "Other" Federalists, 1787–1788*. Indianapolis, IN: Liberty Fund, 1998.

Shevory, Thomas C., ed. *John Marshall's Achievement: Law, Politics, and Constitutional Interpretation*. New York: Greenwood Press, 1989.

Siegel, Stephen A. "Rebalancing Professor Ely's Reappraisal of the Marshall Court and Property Rights." *John Marshall Law Review* 33, no. 4 (2000): 1165–73.

Simmons, A. John. *Justification and Legitimacy*. New York: Cambridge University Press, 2001.

Simon, James F. *What Kind of Nation: Thomas Jefferson, John Marshall, and the Epic Struggle to Create a United States*. New York: Simon and Schuster, 2002.

Singer, Brian C. J. "Cultural versus Contractual Nations: Rethinking their Opposition." *History and Theory* 35, no. 3 (1996): 309–37.

Skinner, Quentin. *The Foundations of Modern Political Thought*. 2 vols. Cambridge: Cambridge University Press, 1978.

———. "The Republican Ideal of Political Liberty." *Machiavelli and Republicanism*, edited by Gisela Bock, Quentin Skinner, and Maurizio Viroli, 293–309. New York: Cambridge University Press, 1990.

———. *Liberty Before Liberalism*. New York: Cambridge University Press, 1998.

———. "The Idea of Negative Liberty: Machiavellian and Modern Perspectives." In *Visions of Politics*, vol. 2, by Quentin Skinner, 186–212. Cambridge: Cambridge University Press, 2002.

———. "Freedom as the Absence of Arbitrary Power." In *Republicanism and Political Theory*, edited by Cécile Laborde and John Maynor, 83–101. Malden, MA: Blackwell, 2008.

Sloan, Cliff, and David McKean. *The Great Decision: Jefferson, Adams, Marshall, and the Battle for the Supreme Court*. New York: Public Affairs, 2009.

Slotkin, Richard. *Gunfighter Nation: The Myth of the Frontier in Twentieth-Century America*. New York: Atheneum, 1992.

Smith, Anthony D. *National Identity*. Reno: University of Nevada Press, 1991.

Smith, Jean Edward. *John Marshall: Definer of a Nation*. New York: Henry Holt, 1996.

Smith, Peter J. "The Marshall Court and the Originalist's Dilemma." *Minnesota Law Review* 90 (2006): 612–77.

Snowiss, Sylvia. *Judicial Review and the Law of the Constitution*. New Haven, CT: Yale University Press, 1990.

Spinner-Halev, Jeff. *The Boundaries of Citizenship: Race, Ethnicity, and Nationality in the Liberal State*. Baltimore, MD: Johns Hopkins University Press, 1994.

Stites, Francis N. *John Marshall: Defender of the Constitution*. Boston, MA: Little, Brown and Co., 1981.

Storing, Herbert. *What the Anti-Federalists Were For*. Chicago: University of Chicago Press, 1981.

Strauber, Ira L. *Neglected Policies: Constitutional Law and Legal Commentary as Civic Education*. Durham, NC: Duke University Press, 2002.

Strauss, David A. "Common Law, Common Ground, and Jefferson's Principle." *Yale Law Journal* 112, no. 7 (2003): 1717–55.

———. *The Living Constitution*. New York: Oxford University Press, 2010.

———. "Legitimacy, 'Constitutional Patriotism,' and the Common Law Constitution." *Harvard Law Review Forum* 126 (2012): 50–55.

Strauss, Leo. *Natural Right and History*. Chicago: University of Chicago Press, 1965.

Strickland, Rennard. "The Tribal Struggle for Indian Sovereignty: The Story of the Cherokee Cases." In *Race Law Stories*, edited by Rachel F. Moran and Devon W. Carbado. New York: Thomson Reuters, 2008.

Swindler, William F. "Politics as Law: The Cherokee Cases." *American Indian Law Review* 3, no. 1 (1975): 7–20.

Tamir, Yael. *Liberal Nationalism*. Princeton, NJ: Princeton University Press, 1993.

Tate, Adam. "James Madison and State Sovereignty, 1780–1781." *American Political Thought* 2, no. 2 (2013): 174–97.

Tushnet, Mark V., ed. *Arguing Marbury v. Madison*. Stanford, CA: Stanford University Press, 2005.

Unger, Harlow Giles. *John Marshall: The Chief Justice Who Saved The Nation*. Philadelphia: De Capo Press, 2014.

Urbinati, Nadia. "Competing for Liberty: The Republican Critique of Democracy." *American Political Science Review* 106, no. 3 (2012): 607–21.

Vanberg, Georg. "Legislative-Judicial Relations: A Game-Theoretic Approach to Constitutional Review." *American Journal of Political Science* 45, no. 2 (2001): 346–61.

Viroli, Maurizio. *Republicanism*. Translated by Antony Shugaar. New York: Hill and Wang, 2002.

Voegelin, Eric. *The New Science of Politics*. Chicago: University of Chicago Press, 1987.

Wallace, Anthony F. C. *The Long, Bitter Trail: Andrew Jackson and the Indians*. New York: Macmillan, 1993.

Warren, Charles. *The Supreme Court in United States History*. 3 vols. Boston: Little, Brown and Co., 1922.

Watson, Blake A. "John Marshall and Indian Land Rights: A Historical Rejoinder to the Claim of 'Universal Recognition' of the Doctrine of Discovery." *Seton Hall Law Review* 36, no. 2 (2006): 481–549.

———. "The Impact of the American Doctrine of Discovery on Native Land Rights in Australia, Canada, and New Zealand." *Seattle University Law Review* 34, no. 2 (2011): 507–51.

Weingast, Barry R. "The Political Foundations of Democracy and the Rule of Law." *American Political Science Review* 91, no. 2 (1997): 245–63.

White, G. Edward. *The Marshall Court and Cultural Change.* New York: Oxford University Press, 1991.

Whittington, Keith. *Political Foundations of Judicial Supremacy.* Princeton, NJ: Princeton University Press, 2007.

Wilkins, David E. *American Indian Sovereignty and the U. S. Supreme Court: The Masking of Justice.* Austin: University of Texas Press, 1997.

Wilkinson, Charles F. *American Indians, Time, and Law: Native Societies in a Modern Constitutional Democracy.* New Haven, CT: Yale University Press, 1987.

Williams, Robert A. *Like a Loaded Weapon: The Rehnquist Court, Indian Rights, and the Legal History of Racism in America.* Minneapolis: University of Minnesota Press, 2005.

Willis, Hugh. "The Doctrine of Sovereignty under the United States Constitution." *Virginia Law Review* 15, no. 4 (1929): 437–75.

Wilson, Bradford P., and Ken Masugi, eds. *The Supreme Court and American Constitutionalism.* Lanham, MD: Rowman & Littlefield, 1998.

Wilson, Woodrow. *Constitutional Government in the United States.* New York: Columbia University Press, 1908.

Winterer, Caroline. *The Culture of Classicism: Ancient Greece and Rome in American Intellectual Life, 1780–1910.* Baltimore, MD: Johns Hopkins University Press, 2002.

Wolfe, Christopher. "John Marshall & Constitutional Law." *Polity* 15, no. 1 (1989): 5–25.

Wood, Gordon S. *The Creation of the American Republic, 1776–1787.* Chapel Hill: University of North Carolina Press, 1969.

———. "The Intellectual Origins of the American Constitution." *National Forum* 64, no. 4 (1984): 5–8.

———. *Empire of Liberty: A History of the Early Republic, 1789–1815.* New York: Oxford University Press, 2009.

Xenos, Nicholas. "Civic Nationalism: Oxymoron." *Critical Review* 10, no. 2 (1996): 213–31.

Yack, Bernard. "The Myth of the Civic Nation." *Critical Review* 10, no. 2 (1996): 193–211.

Yarbrough, Jean. "The Constitution and Character: The Missing Critical Principle?" In *To Form a More Perfect Union: The Critical Ideas of the Constitution,* edited by Herman Belz, Ronald Hoffman, and Peter J. Albert, 217–49. Charlottesville: University of Virginia Press, 1992.

Zuckert, Michael P. *The Natural Rights Republic: Studies in the Foundation of the American Political Tradition.* Notre Dame, IN: University of Notre Dame Press, 1996.

Index